I0168802

Choosing Purpose & Passion in Christ Over Self

by Gwen Cobb Burno

CREATED TO BE: Choosing Purpose & Passion in Christ Over Self

ISBN: 979-8-9872779-0-4

Cover and interior design by Marji Laine
Published by:

Roaring Lambs Publishing
17110 Dallas Parkway, Suite 260
Dallas, TX 75248

Printed in the United States of America

Dedication Page

This book is dedicated to:

Grandma
who saw me when I couldn't see myself.
Your kind gentle words continue to echo in my ears.
I still cry for you – over 20 years later.

And Mom
who refused to let me shrivel away in my failures
but insisted that I keep going.

And Rowland, Jeremy, Mikaela, Kiersten
my true love and joy.
Your presence has shaped my
relationship with God
in unimaginable countless ways.
Thanks for being my loving and supportive family.

Contents

Introduction

Once upon a time I thought my most important relationship was with the people I saw, touched, laughed, cried, missed, and enjoyed. My focus was on investing and building upon all that belonged in the physical world.

Personally, the plan was set—get an education, provide for myself financially, marry well, give birth, and pass down my philosophies. As soon as I set out to execute this overly simplified plan, the threads began to unravel into a frayed mess. What happened? How could my thoughts and visions betray me in such an abrasive way? Many years later I discovered the answer to these questions.

In all my meticulous plans, one crucial essential piece was missing …

GOD

Who knew that:

- God cared about what I thought?
- God wanted to be number one in my plans?
- God created me with His unique purpose and plan?

- God created me for Himself first?
- God chose me before I was formed in my mother's womb?
- God did not tolerate another god before Him, including 'self'?
- God desired an intimate relationship with me?

Did you know this about God? I certainly didn't.

God pursued me until His point was clear. My insecurities coupled with a disconnect to God resembled puzzle pieces strewn all over the table. Mass confusion. God and His truths shed light onto my desperate situation. I learned that the fastest guaranteed way to failure was by omitting God and trusting in myself.

This book, a labor of love, is to help others not to go it alone. The Bible provides numerous lessons to teach us how to interact with God. I include ten chapters that focus on 'how to be' in establishing and protecting your most critical relationship. The world is demanding and vying for our attention constantly, but look beyond the physical. Real sustaining independence and true freedom exist in the spiritual world, the place where plans align with purpose.

Denying self is not an easy feat, but nonnegotiable if a life well-lived is the goal. Jesus says, "he who loves his life loses it, and he who hates his life in this world will keep it to life eternal" (Jn 12:25). Created to Be is written to highlight practices that will cause you to fall in love with God and never want to leave or isolate Him.

Enjoy the read! And remember that we are created to be in pursuit of and resting securely with a loving, gracious, merciful God all the days of our lives.

Blessings, my friend
Gwen

Chapter 1
Be Knowledgeable

Read Luke 24:13-35

> *And behold, two of them were going that very day to a village named Emmaus, which was about seven miles from Jerusalem. And they were talking with each other about all these things which had taken place. While they were talking and discussing, Jesus Himself approached and began traveling with them. But their eyes were prevented from recognizing Him.*
>
> *Luke 24:13-16 (NASB)*

Two men walking along a familiar road experienced one of the most uncommon occurrences in history. Cleophas and an unnamed man had each other for company as they attempted to decipher the recent happenings. The times were troubling and disappointing. People were unsettled for various reasons.

The Atmosphere

Israel's interface with Jesus, their long-awaited Messiah, was met with trepidation. The people desired deliverance from oppressive Rome by a mighty conqueror. For centuries, God's people had been anticipating His arrival, a military hero like David who would forever sit on the throne. Jesus wasn't what they expected, even though He spoke with authority. Fears and worries filled them rather than the enthusiasm one would expect.

There was a part of Israel enamored with His miracles that followed Jesus. Though He kept to the outskirts of towns, they could see His miraculous might. Even up to His great entry into Jerusalem, they believed Him to be a military hero in the making. Sadly, the appeal faded as the rise to power that they anticipated failed to appear, and many walked away.

The Pharisees, chief priests, and others were skeptical to receive Jesus the Nazarene as a Messiah, some even hostile. Feeling pressured, the religious establishment sought to uphold the integrity of the Old Testament, particularly the Law, refusing to consider the possibility that He might be more than the nobody of consequence they believed him to be.

Of course, Jesus, was not intimidated by them. He challenged the religious leadership in their knowledge and righteousness.

It was a no-go for the Pharisees, though. It should have been easy for the religious sect, astute in the

Scriptures, to accept Jesus the Nazarene, but His questioning of their motives and their false piety nipped at their pride.

Tensions arose within the chosen people. The common ground was a need for a Messiah, but Jesus was rejected by authority as the prime candidate for this role. The chief priests and others were committed to a mission which upheld the Law given by Moses. Regrettably, the Law became muddled with additional requirements intended to ensure remaining in good standing before a holy God and avoiding wrath. Man's addition to God's provision contributed chaos and confusion. Unfortunately, not all good intentions equate to goodness. These measures created unnecessary and unrealistic burdens for the people.

Jesus challenged those who added requirements to the Law. As I mentioned before, He was not the anticipated Messiah in the eyes of some who held powerful positions. So much so, the vengeance did not cease until the cross was erected and the burial took place.

The chief priests with tunnel vision and hardened hearts were successful in accomplishing a hideous act in the name of satisfying an angry god, their god. It is safe to conclude that the chief priests' god, according to their actions, condoned murder in a manner that even Rome, the crucifixion originator, recognized as deplorable and despicable. "Cursed is everyone who hangs on a tree" (Galatians 3:13, Deuteronomy 21:23, NASB). was sufficient motivation for the priests to insist on that type of death, aligning themselves with their own oppressors.

The point was to create a public spectacle and put an end to any hopeful thread that spun throughout the community. Kill the hope, redirect the focus, and retain control. Fortunately, those who exercise misguided power have no influence on God Almighty, Maker of heaven and earth.

Cleophas and his friend very likely heard of the crucifixion of Jesus that morning or early afternoon. I can imagine how they and the rest of His followers stayed in the periphery, hardly able to believe what they were seeing, as Messiah, who had proven Himself to be the Son of God, was hung on a Roman cross until He was dead.

Along the Road

And this is where Cleophas and his friend found themselves, clearly shaken by recent events. They walked and discussed the matters with broken hearts. They had such hope that Jesus was the One. His words had been like manna to His starving people. He'd been mighty in deed and spoken with such authority in the sight of God and all the people (19).

All the time that they had spent with him, had listened to his words, he'd shown such extraordinary compassion to the people. So much more than they had seen from anyone else. He seemed to have a mission to serve, and in that vein he healed, taught, and clarified all that they had assumed about God.

He even spent time with obvious sinners. He made a beeline to the untouchables, like an adulterous Samaritan woman, lepers, the lame, and even tax collectors. The welcome wagon was available for anyone in a helpless state. Was this actually the way that God's Kingdom would be? A place for all mankind to have a relationship with God the Father?

For these two men, a moment in time arrived when finally an opportunity presented itself to breathe a sigh of relief.

We see Jesus joining the two men on the road to Emmaus and engaging them in conversation with a question. In slang terms, "Whatcha talking about?" Jesus made a point to interact with them based on their current actions and setting.

Whatcha talking about?

This was a clever opening to reveal the hearts of the two men. Their hearts were consumed with sadness and disappointment. Also, the men were astonished that the gentleman before them appeared to be clueless of the latest news. Even those just visiting Jerusalem were aware of what was going on. The two men enlightened their guest concerning Jesus' death with illuminating details. It was the third day, yet the two men responded as if it were yesterday. But the ordeal did not end on the cross. There were women in their company who reported an empty tomb and a vision of angels who stated that Jesus was alive.

Jesus, true to form, set out to unscramble the letters for these men in order to perfect their knowledge and understanding. However, it was not before Jesus called the men foolish and slow. After calling a spade a spade, Jesus proceeded on His mission to reveal truth.

He explained that the Messiah would suffer and be resurrected according to Moses and the prophets. I can imagine He told them, "Do not lose heart. Do not be without understanding. Know the Scriptures."

After all, the Scriptures were preserved as testimony and evidence to safeguard and lead Israel to the Messiah. God was true to the words echoed through His prophets.

Being ever faithful, God would be true to His Word and not let those who trust in Him falter. Jesus in compassion and patience offered the saddened hearts hope again through knowledge.

The two men, so captivated by Jesus' teachings, refused to let go of Him. "Stay with us, for it is getting toward evening, and the day is now nearly over" (Luke 24:29 NASB). The two men craved more of Jesus, more of His time, more of His words. They found comfort in Jesus during their distress. Jesus graciously accepted the offer to stay.

Continuing fellowship with the two men, Jesus reclined at the table. He took the bread, blessed it, broke it, and served it. How fitting for the Bread of Life to serve Himself to others at the table. Jesus satisfied the hunger and thirst of those who were desperate for His nourishment.

The men responded exactly the same way simultaneously. Their eyes opened to the truth. They recognized Jesus.

And at that moment, Jesus vanished from their sight, His mission complete. Jesus conveyed clearly that He was the resurrection and the life according to the words of the prophets.

The hope that had kindled minimal knowledge was not in vain. Hearts once consumed by sadness now burned with fire. "Did not our hearts burn within us while He was speaking and explaining to us?" (Luke 24:32 NASB). An open, burning heart will spread wildfires as others come and ignite from its flame.

Jesus encountered two broken-hearted men and left them burning with blazing inferno intensity.

The Savior joined the two men on the road to Emmaus not for mere exercise and companionship, although they benefited greatly from His presence. He joined with intent and purpose to open the minds of the two downtrodden travelers. The highlight of the time together was not the walk together. Jesus connected the walking together with understanding.

The two men had a great need, redemption for their beloved nation. Jesus recognized that need and realized other needs as well, personal redemption and knowledge. The men needed to believe in the words of the prophets in order to identify the Redeemer. As long as the men failed to recognize or understand, they remained in a state of despair.

Once Jesus explained and filled their minds with true knowledge, their hearts burned. Embers were lit, past misunderstandings clarified, and hope restored. Truth stirred in the hearts coupled with an awakened love and passion.

Through knowledge given by the only One who

really knew the whole story, they were no longer disappointed by recent disturbing events. In fact, their Redeemer lived and demonstrated incomparable power by overcoming death on a cross, a sealed tomb, and an impenetrable security team.

After returning from those horrific events, Jesus resumed His mission to teach others the Truth. Jesus went to amazing lengths deterred by no earthly forces in order to satisfy and please the Father by carrying out His will. This profound understanding gives a fresh appreciation to John 1:14, "the Word became flesh and dwelt among us." The Word, the living Word, came to reside on earth in order to bring light and understanding to those who were blinded by ignorance. The Father, Son, and Holy Spirit want the creation to be equipped with knowledge.

To know God is to love Him. The more we know, the more we will love Him.

Why? To know God is to love Him. The more we know, the more we will love Him. Since we will never know God fully, this is an eternal process. It is best to get started now.

Shattered Hope

I sat across the table from a young lady whose eyes

were filled with streaming tears; a heart overwhelmed by frustrations. She expressed that she did not know what or who to believe anymore. She was receiving conflicting accounts of the Word. Her faith was shattered with frayed hope hanging by a thread. Her conclusion was to give up on God.

I prayed for the right words. So much was at stake. I identified with her pain and validated that many use God's Word for selfish gain and promote personal agendas. This tactic to distort or masquerade truth can be traced in history throughout time. People have suffered mercilessly under this distortion.

Entrusting personal faith to someone else is risky business. My message to the young lady was that God would never give up on her so she should not give up on Him. She needed to give up relying on others.

This was a person who was reluctant to search the Scriptures for herself. With a lack of personal understanding, she was relying on her own judgment and wisdom and easily fell prey to an alternative message.

That message was then and will always be "God is not enough. God does not love you. He will never satisfy you. He does not keep His promises." This message leads even sincere believers to feel aimless and without hope.

Interestingly, God led her to be in the presence of someone who feasted on Scripture and considered this activity as a non-negotiable commitment. A blessing for her as she would be fed Truth from God.

Her choice, along with any believer presented with the Truth, would be whether to digest the feast set before her or not.

"The knowledge of the Holy One is understanding."
Proverbs 9:10b (NASB)

Contemplation Corner

1. How would you describe your knowledge of God?

2. Do you seek God on a daily basis? If so, how? If not, why not?

3. What difference has the knowledge of God made in your life?

4. How has your heart burned for God recently?

Chapter 2
Be Mindful

Read Genesis 3:1-13

> *I am no longer in the world; and yet they themselves are in the world, and I come to You. Holy Father, keep them in Your name, the name which You have given Me, that they may be one even as We are.*
>
> John 17:11

Mindfulness sounds great in theory, but in practice well that is an altogether different thought. With researchers telling us that we are capable of 30,000 thoughts each day, we are guaranteed to be swept away by one of the misfits that sneak in to carouse us into daydreaming or some type of aimless wandering.

You know the type. One moment you are productive, the next moment you are thinking about the laundry, checking emails, texting or reading the latest celebrity news. Forty-five minutes later, you're jolted back to reality, feeling defeated because the willpower was not there to send the misfit away sooner.

For this very reason, mindfulness is a practice which

requires a constant mental check-in to ensure that you are focusing on what is necessary for that particular moment.

Mindfulness was once a way of life, not a practice. In order to understand better, let us return to our origin where it all began in an idyllic setting, the Garden of Eden.

After marveling over God's omnipotence during the creative process in the first few pages of the Book of Genesis, we discover Adam and Eve enjoying the marvelous outcome. The Garden of Eden conjures imagery such as fulfillment, contentment, joy, and the list continues with words that spark ultimate gratification and admiration. Some of the striking points of the Garden derived from its all-sufficiency. Incomparable beauty was captured in a perfectly orchestrated garden. The place encouraged rest as well as work without stress. Bountiful provision lay within hand's-reach, eliminating the need to worry.

In addition to these perks of living in Eden, Adam and Eve thrived in perfect companionship. They reveled in a committed relationship in which strife and discord did not exist. Their ideal relationship never experienced jealousy. God never advised Adam and Eve not to go to bed angry, and they didn't need help to determine their love languages. They spoke each other's language fluently and flawlessly. Adam and Eve never conceived of attending marriage counseling or a weekend retreat.

Today's marriages are so far removed from this original design. Sin has entered and perverted marriage in such a manner that reduces its meaning to one person making the other happy. Failure to accomplish this overwhelming expectation leads to a downward spiral into constant bickering and disappointment. God initiated holy matrimony intentionally, for us to be aware of the ever-present position held by God in our marriages. God lost that placement to an ill-equipped intruder.

Self.

Sadly, we continue to fall prey to selfish demands that seek to please and uplift us through prioritizing our feelings and emotions. Unfortunately, since God is the only one capable of satisfying His creation, we move away from God in search of our answer.

The answer that we crave will always be found nearby. There is no need to wander far away in search of answers or identity. The Creator, the Master Designer, holds the copyright to the intellectual property which contains the answers that we seek. And He is always close to us. If only, we will recognize His omnipresence.

The Lord is near to all who call upon Him, to all who call upon Him in truth. He will fulfill the desire of those

> *who fear Him; He will also hear their cry and will save them.*
>
> *Psalm 145:18-19 (NASB)*

The pinnacle of the Garden is the unspoiled fellowship that existed amongst God, Adam, and Eve. God who walked through the Garden freely and openly yearned to spend time with Adam and Eve, an event written as if an ordinary activity—ordinary in the sense of regular occurrence, but extraordinary in every other manner. God, in His fullness of glory and holiness, welcomed and desired to be in the presence of created human beings without any barriers.

Adam and Eve who were privileged to enjoy His majestic presence submitted in perfect mindfulness, fully aware of the true meaning of the moment. This environment was free from pesty distractions. It was absolute pleasure with minds entirely placated while enjoying each other and God according to the original creative purposes.

What do you really want?

Imagine that I am sitting with you this very moment. We just completed reading how much God enjoyed being in the Garden with Adam and Eve. My most pressing question to you would be, what do you really want in life?

After dismissing the superficial answers which lay at the surface, like a new house, car, money, prestige, etc., your thoughts would probably meander to more meaningful responses. Springing up from the depths of your essence would be expressions of muffled cravings for a peace of mind, joy, love, and healing. You have discovered the reality that the rat race benefits the rats only and leaves you exhausted physically and mentally. You prefer a setting in which you do not need to be taught how to meditate and breathe. Your wish is to inhale and exhale naturally and appreciate the surrounding beauty simply because your mind has permission to slow down and contemplate. You yearn for a relationship with time in which each moment is refreshing instead of a harassing intimidating foe always working against you. Freedom to express your creativity and live unashamedly according to natural gifts embedded within is your deepest desire. In the crevice of your being, you long for those who belong to you to experience similarly.

> No purpose or mission is worthy unless grounded in gratitude and correlates to God's creative agenda.

This is a pure blissful and harmonious existence. And if we are honest, we all want it.

In sharing what you really want, I would listen for

words that identify with your purpose and mission. No purpose or mission is worthy unless grounded in gratitude and correlates to God's creative agenda. Your words, emotions, and sighs of exasperation indicate that what you really want is to include the Lord, the one who made it all possible in your daily affairs on a moment-by-moment basis. Your heartfelt longing is to be mindful of the presence of God. You do not wish to relegate God to Sunday morning or the end of your exhausting day.

We want our minds to reach and remain at that peaceful, calm state just like Adam and Eve, wholly present with God. Even if for just once in your lifetime, you would give anything to experience a physical one-on-one interaction with God.

Just once, you would choose to walk by sight and not by faith.

Your excitement for this possibility is akin to a little kid in the toy store waiting in line for a turn with Santa. The only difference is there is no wait. And there is no line. Only an open invitation with the Lord who loves unconditionally without time constraints. Hopefully, even the thought of this interaction brings joy and tears of elation to your heart.

Or do these words stir an *if only*?

- If only, this was my reality.
- If only, you knew my circumstances.

- If only, I was worthy.
- If only, I could allow myself to dream again; feel again; hope again.

Once upon a time is the beginning of fairy tales. This story does not begin this way. This story opens with, "in the beginning God . . ." Any story that leads with God who creates in six days and rests on the seventh is trustworthy of cradling and protecting hopes.

Based on the above description, our deepest longings are for the times that Adam and Eve enjoyed in the Garden of Eden before sin entered. If we allow ourselves to be vulnerable with truth, we will admit that we want heaven. We want heaven right now. We want heaven on earth. We want things to return to the way it was in the Garden of Eden. And we will do anything within our own power and strength to make this happen.

Goodness belongs to God, and God alone.

Our determination includes forging a strong bond with persistence in insisting that the world behaves in a manner that always brings good to us. Then, our hearts are filled with disappointment when the world does not deliver this goodness demanded from it.

Goodness belongs to God, and God alone.

No matter how many attempts, we will never extract

a smooth sweet taste from a fresh firm lemon. It is simply an unrealistic expectation. Expecting goodness, especially lifelong grace and mercy, from the world is utterly ridiculous.

God is good as evidenced through His creativity. If only we mastered and held firm to this truth. Then our questions about God's goodness would be non-existent, such as:

- Why does God permit suffering?
- Why did God allow the young child to die?
- Why didn't God intervene when I needed Him the most?

Our tainted misunderstandings skew our minds to believe that God abandoned us in this fallen world without adequate protection or defensive gear, left us to our own vices.

God does not take pleasure in our falters. Consistent throughout the Bible is the promise that God is with us.

> *The Lord is the one who goes ahead of you; He will be with you. He will not fail you or forsake you. Do not fear or be dismayed.*
>
> *Deuteronomy 31:8 (NASB)*

However as soon as we shed a tear or sense a crisis in the making, God receives the blame for the actions of a world that is in blatant opposition to Him. He even takes the blame for our lack of faith and still chooses not to give up on His creation. And yet, at the highpoint of our stubbornness, He remains good to His creation who demonstrates an inept attitude toward faithfulness or committing to the plan intended to grant the heart's desire which is to return to the Garden of Eden.

> *The Lord, the Lord God, compassionate and gracious, slow to anger, and abounding in lovingkindness and truth; who keeps lovingkindness for thousands, who forgives iniquity, transgression and sin . . .*
>
> *Exodus 34:6b-7 (NASB)*

God is wholly perfect in His knowledge and plans for the present and future. His intention is never to leave us alone but to remain active in our lives.

> *For the eyes of the Lord move to and fro throughout the earth that He may strongly support those whose heart is completely His.*
>
> *2 Chronicles 16:9 (NASB).*

What Happened to Disrupt My Joy?

Unfortunately, this pure and unadulterated fellowship that causes our hearts to long for the same interaction came to a screeching halt once deception entered the Garden. Adam and Eve enjoyed access to

God and admired His magnificence and character so much so that they desired those qualities for themselves. They were introduced to the idea of coveting by desiring the qualities that distinguished the Creator from the created. Desiring to be like God was appealing, but to act on an impulsive disobedient thought delivered grave consequences for Adam, Eve, and the generations to follow. We suffer as a result of an undisciplined mind that failed to take captive a destructive thought and cause it to submit to obedience.

Mindfulness is when the data in the head connects to the heart forming an impenetrable bond which leads to commitment.

The divine instructions were given concisely without room for misinterpretation.

> *From the tree of the knowledge of good and evil you shall not eat, for in the day that you eat from it you will surely die.*
>
> *Genesis 2:17 (NASB)*

These were the words spoken to Adam but clearly relayed to Eve. Later, she reiterated the boundaries to the snake with added enhancements,

> *From the fruit of the trees of the garden we may eat; but from the fruit of the tree which is in the middle of the*

garden, God has said, "You shall not eat from it or touch it, or you will die."'

Genesis 3:2-3 (NASB)

Eve memorized the command and recited it confidently. However, she revealed a disconnect between her understanding and God's instructions. She taught us that rote memory is not the same as belief. Eve was capable of storing and retrieving data, but commitment resides in the heart.

Mindfulness is when the data in the head connects to the heart forming an impenetrable bond which leads to commitment.

God's presence and divine qualities are attractive enough to draw others to want to know and be like Him. The difference between a healthy and depraved mindset is the realization that humans are incapable of being God. Humans are fashioned to please God, not be God. At no point in our life story will we ever become His equal.

If you think about it, do you really want to serve a God whose knowledge is comparable to yours? I need my God to be above and beyond my capabilities so that I may always view Him as a trustworthy source who knows and wants the very best for me.

Being the captain of my own ship and the master of my fate mean that I will always be hitched at the dock. I am too fearful to go it alone as I do not have a clue pertaining to the destination. I am stuck on which direction will lead to the best future. My mind cannot conceive the plans that God has for me. "Things which eye has not seen and ear has not heard, and which have not entered the heart of man, all that God has prepared for those who love Him" (1Cor. 2:9 NASB). I will underestimate and fall short each time I attempt to know what is best.

Examine your life and list the experiences that occurred without your intervening, completely unexplainable by self-efforts. Unless you are a person who prescribes to coincidences or luck, you will be shocked at the countless times God has led you each step of the way. Identify the experiences that you have been willing to give yourself sole credit for making happen.

In all honesty, this is a futile exercise. Let us just give God glory for the great things He has done for us.

The created, that is, Adam and Eve, failed to respect the creative order and diminished the need to worship God. Satan, who first coveted God's qualities, enticed Adam and Eve to take a bite of the forbidden fruit in order to become like God.

People are often taken aback by evil. With careful observation, we realize that evil is simply doing what evil is supposed to do. In other words, evil carries out its agenda. We should not be surprised when we witness it in action. Satan, a masterful trickster, saw an opportunity to ensnare humanity by adhering to deceptive practices.

> *The serpent said to the woman, "You surely will not die! For God knows that in the day you eat from it your eyes will be opened, and you will be like God, knowing good and evil."*
>
> *Genesis 3:4-5 (NASB)*

Satan's offer led Eve to believe that she had been walking around with her eyes closed to something greater within her grasp. Satan not only appealed to Eve's physical eyes, but her mind's eye as well. The mind's eye is the place in which visions and dreams take place. Somehow, Eve connected to the tempting offer and acted upon it. She saw something in her mind that suggested how much more wonderful life would be if she was like God.

We must remember that Adam and Eve were living the perfect life already. Eve permitted herself to believe the impossible. Her mind became fixated upon improving upon what God provided. Could Eve have been thinking this lustfully enticing thought, "Does the forbidden fruit mean that God would be forced to share His position, glory or essence with me?"

Satan presented God as one who knows good and evil. The truth masqueraded in this statement is God's awareness of evil, yet He remains good. Humans are not privy to boast the same claim. Humanity has come to know the difference between good and evil, but the ability to choose good over evil through our own initiative eludes us like a leaky bucket holding water.

> *There is none righteous, not even one; there is none who understands, there is none who seeks for God; all have turned aside, together they have become useless; there is none who does good, there is not even one.*
>
> *Romans 3:10-12 (NASB)*

Regardless of how hard I attempt to generate good apart from Jesus Christ, my efforts are as relevant as a check returned for insufficient funds—worthless.

Paul describes this good versus evil battle in Romans as waging war against the law of my mind and making me a prisoner of the law of sin which is in my members. Paul labeled himself as a wretched man in bondage to the body of death. He recognized that his only means to freedom was sent by God through His Son. Only through Jesus' obedience to the Father was Paul able to use his mind to serve the law of God (Romans 7:23-25).

Satan's wildly successful plan of attack was to challenge the mind with a mixture of truths and lies. He distorted the truth just enough to cause Eve to question and doubt. During this process, the forbidden fruit appeared more desirable as God and His holiness faded into the background. God's words, once the epitome of wisdom, were reduced to a mere suggestion.

The plan of attack has not changed. And yet, we continue to be lured by false promises to become greater than or equal to God. Satan in his crafty cleverness uplifts God and His Word and pokes around until he discovers weak spots in us. Satan wants to persuade humans that God cannot be trusted and that an undercover liar and accuser is more trustworthy. And we follow the evil one blindly into his dark world to be held hostage and used for his bidding. We spend a lifetime searching and contributing an exorbitant amount of resources to capture this false claim to be like God. Jesus' teachings are precise in shining light into darkness. His followers are mindful in choosing the well-lit path.

Genesis is very clear in outlining the divine order. God is sovereign. Mankind are beloved companions to Him. All else on Earth are subject to mankind. There's no high-level math or physics in God's order.

The requirements for diminishing evil's impact rests solely within accepting God's sovereignty.

> *Thus says the Lord, the Holy One of Israel, and his Maker: Ask Me about the things to come concerning My sons, and you shall commit to Me the work of My hands. It is I who made the earth and created man upon it. I*

stretched out the heavens with My hands and I ordained all their host.

Isaiah 45:11-12 (NASB)

Man was not present, participating alongside God or assisting during the creative process. Man was nonexistent until his appointed time to join the marvelous creation for a specific purpose.

The word, purpose, is a popular two-cent word associated with personal and professional development these days.

So allow me to get personal. Apart from understanding God and your beginnings as stated in Genesis, you are spinning your wheel into an empty, shallow existence.

Purpose-driven statements have become very popular. They usually sound something like, your purpose is:

- to live your best life.
- to accumulate material wealth for your satisfaction, comfort, and delight.
- to be the best version of you.

What is the common denominator in each statement? You. This is the evil one's message, infiltrating again and again to remove the focus from God and place it on yourself.

How can your purpose statement be meaningful and fulfilling apart from your Creator? It would be the same as asking a nursing infant to thrive apart from his mother, the sole source of nutrients. God is the Provider of all sustenance necessary to live.

> *And my God will supply all your needs according to His riches in glory in Christ Jesus.*
>
> *Philippians 4:19 (NASB)*

Any life-purpose statement must be penned in God's love and mercy that He demonstrates moment by moment each day.

- How does life unfold within the context of God's love and mercy?
- How do actions draw others to admire and love God?

To be driven to live purposefully is to point others to God, Creator, for praise and adoration. In making a commitment to know God, there is an enduring purpose that will consider each individual's unique gifts and talents. These blessings were intended to be returned to the Maker for use according to His pleasure.

Don't let anyone with a large following and charismatic message lead you away from your Creator. Stay close and be mindful of His presence.

We quote Jeremiah 29:11, "'For I know the plans that I have for you,' declares the Lord, 'plans for welfare and not for calamity to give you a future and a hope.'" But we overlook verse twelve, "Then you will call upon Me and come and pray to Me, and I will listen to you."

Why is it necessary to call, come and pray?

So that we can understand the plan. God promises to listen to us and assure us with comforting guidance that fulfilling our life purpose is part of His plan. God has the plan. Our role is to meet with God for instructions on executing the plan.

Will I receive the complete plan for my life with one visit to God? No, I would probably faint and become paralyzed if I knew what lay ahead. So, God feeds me what I need to know for the moment.

God practices mindfulness too.

There are times when my husband is driving, and while we are very close to our destination, he does not have enough information to know for certain. He refuses to consult with Google Maps or Waze for assistance. So, I quietly reach for my cell phone and search for the address. Eventually with guidance, we reach our destination. Sometimes this is a smooth process. Other times there may be pushback. Regardless, I continue to consult a trustworthy source.

God is far more knowledgeable than Waze or

Google Maps. Choosing not to consult the Master Planner who has a vested interest in our ultimate arrival is an avoidable offense.

Defeating the Snake

Through the one act between Eve and the snake, we learn of the covetous nature of the evil one who employed deceptive means to distort God's words and trapped Adam and Eve into following him. Satan constructed a convincing plea from his intrinsic interests to be God. In order for him to appear to be like God, he needed God's followers to reorient their allegiance toward him and his will.

Satan still needs followers to build his kingdom and carry out his deceptive plan which contradicts God's kingdom but never rivals in power and strength. If there are no takers or interests in identifying with evil, then there are no followers.

Let's take that a step further—a weakened satanic kingdom is less effective in soliciting others to believe half-truths. According to the end of the biblical story in Revelation, one day there will be no takers aligning with the evil one.

Hallelujah!

> *When the woman saw that the tree was good for food and that it was a delight to the eyes, and that the tree was desirable to make one wise, she took from its fruit and ate; and she gave also to her husband with her, and he ate.*
> *Genesis 3:6 (NASB)*

Each time I teach this Scripture in Bible study, the men and women blame each other immediately. I pause and allow the banter to express itself fully with laughter and debate. Usually, the women win the argument probably because we overwhelm the argument with more words and the men want peace when they get home.

We tend to think our decision-making skills and disdain for temptations would yield different results if we were substitutes in the Garden during the snake's offer.

Wishful thinking at its finest.

Adam and Eve represent humanity. Therefore, we all possess the same nature, with a propensity to sin and walk away from God. If Adam and Eve, who had complete and direct physical access, failed to choose God, then why do we believe that we are strong enough to choose differently? An over-inflated self-image results in this line of thinking.

This is evidence of a depraved mind due to a fallen nature. A depraved mind is incapable of formulating healthy judgments and sound decisions. Paul confirmed this truth in Romans 3:23, "All have sinned and come short of the glory of God."

The difference with a life in Christ is one that chooses to detest sin and takes practical spiritual steps daily as protection from sin's effects.

> Sin, which is a lack of trust in God, and a love for God cannot coexist in my heart peaceably or equitably.

Does this mean that there can be life without sin? Absolutely not. It means that there is an active confession lifestyle in which one will ask for forgiveness regularly. It's important to treat the relationship with God through Jesus Christ as a treasure that requires guarding from any lurking threats or interferences.

I work at this myself, and, trust me, threats come my way often. My husband's job ended and my insecurities concerning the future overtook reason. We bickered because we viewed the future differently. Why didn't I just trust God for provision initially?

My brother died from cancer, and for a brief moment, I wanted to be angry with God for not delivering a miraculous healing. I soon realized that I needed God to survive this loss. I set aside my anger and pled for mercy to be placed over me like a warm blanket to cover my broken heart.

Threats come from all directions to distract and pull me away from God. How many times has the evil one whispered in my ear concerning my children? Countless.

I need God to stand firm and recognize the devil's lies.

Sin, which is a lack of trust in God, and a love for God cannot coexist in my heart peaceably or equitably. It is literally impossible for two opposing foes to share territory without engaging in strife in which one's mission becomes to dethrone the other.

So, my mission is to feed the one I love and starve the one that seeks to destroy me. My feeding comes from filling my mind with God's Word which creates a continuous steady flow of assurance and admiration in my heart.

One of my very dear friends, whom I consider as close as a sister, and I disagreed over coronavirus, of all things. I believe we were both frustrated in the disruption it was causing in our lives and trying to get a handle on it. Well, over breakfast, I had one position on how to protect myself, and she differed to the point that it created tension. I wanted her to be more careful and she wanted me to relax.

Looking back, the enemy was seeking to destroy this relationship. This friendship blossomed from my seminary days. We spent a lot of time taking classes and discussing God together. Of course, the enemy wanted to separate us. We had never fought before, and I felt horrible. I had a choice to feed the enemy's wishes or continue to cling to my godly relationship. I chose to maintain the friendship. And I will choose her every single time because she loves thinking and talking about God.

By choosing godliness, I shut the door on the enemy's entrance to spread seeds of dissension. There was nothing enticing about dissolving our friendship; rather, it highlighted the most appealing areas of our relationship and increased my determination to align with God.

My will to follow God increases as I understand the enemy's plot to destroy and create havoc in my relationships. The Word admonishes to pursue peace at all times with all people (Hebrews 12:14), but it requires deliberate intent to maintain peacefulness with others.

> **Thank God for His grace that overshadows our weaknesses and makes us whole again.**

Satan acquainted Eve with mindful lust the second she shifted her attention to the tree and saw that the fruit really looked good for food and delightful to the eye. How many times in the past had Eve seen or passed the tree without a second glance? Planted in her heart was a desire to obey God. Lust entered through the eyes and influenced Adam and Eve to commit adultery by becoming unfaithful, abandoning God in exchange for a lie. Lust functioned to manipulate the heart to desire that which was meant to destroy. Satan not only infiltrated Eve's eyes, but lust activated in engaging her heart.

> *For from within, out of the heart of men, proceed the evil thoughts, fornications, thefts, murders, adulteries, deeds of coveting and wickedness, as well as deceit, sensuality, envy, slander, pride and foolishness. All these evil things proceed from within and defile the man.*
>
> *Mark 7:21-23 (NASB)*

The evil heart is masterful at creating tremendous havoc in our lives. We propagate lies as if they were truth to promote our own interests. Marriages dissolve and children's lives are impacted negatively. We connive to gain wealth and status. We lust and covet and justify ungodly behaviors for the sake of momentary happiness.

These examples proceed from an evil heart. An evil heart refuses to acknowledge and adhere to the boundaries that protect from offending God.

> *Therefore let us draw near with confidence to the throne of grace, so that we may receive mercy and find grace to help in time of need.*
>
> *Hebrews 4:16 (NASB)*

Thank God for His grace that overshadows our weaknesses and makes us whole again.

God's provisions in the Garden were abundant to appease physically, spiritually, and sensually. The Garden exploded with creativity to mesmerize man's eye and entertain the mind with lush vegetation, rivers, animals, and more, all designed to express God's uniqueness.

Satan presented a different perverted option for Eve to consider. His option spotlighted an opportunity for her to be like God. It was not enough to enjoy and appreciate the provisions through worship and adoration, but somehow a charming false illusion was more intriguing. Eve, seeing with her eye, which is the body part that God created for her to admire Him and His works, was the precise platform that the devil needed to advance his agenda, separate man from God.

With just one bite of a fruit, disobedience entered onto the scene and set a completely different course for humanity.

Satan approaches humanity in the same manner today by appealing to the eye and mind as a means to distract us from our true purpose of being aligned with God.

> *The eye is the lamp of the body; so then if your eye is clear, your whole body will be full of light. But if your eye is bad, your whole body will be full of darkness. If then the light that is in you is darkness, how great is the darkness!*
> *Matthew 6:22-23*

The darkness is great and demands a price to pay that always leads to death. No good thing comes from darkness. Of course, initial pleasure flirts with the flesh and interacts with the mind to reason that the darkness is worth the risk.

The fruit looked good. The first bite was delectable enough for Eve to pass it on to Adam and the consequences became a reality. "Then the eyes of both of them were opened, and they knew that they were naked" (Gen. 3:6).

This practice will fortify your temperament to obedience and lessen your interest in satisfying the flesh.

With open eyes come the first glimpse at sins' effects. Sin diminishes the weight of God's words and justifies destructive behavior while aligning with the enemy.

This is one of the primary reasons to practice mindfulness of God's presence and His Word through consistent immersion. This practice will fortify your temperament to obedience and lessen your interest in satisfying the flesh. Proper focus on Jesus is the exact prescription needed to stay the course and listen to the voice that is unlike man, incapable of lying or misleading.

Satan approached Jesus to entice Him with the same tactics used on Adam and Eve. Satan decided to appeal to Jesus visually and mindfully in order to lay the groundwork for lust and accomplish his goal, create division between Jesus and the Father.

When that didn't work, Satan wanted Jesus to bow down and worship him in an attempt to undermine His relationship with the Father. In Matthew 4:8, Jesus was taken to a mountain and shown glorious kingdoms, specifically to engage the eye. Satan offered these kingdoms to Jesus in exchange for His bowing down and worshiping.

Satan's thinking—if I can trap Jesus with my tactics then I will deliver a major blow to His earthly mission and God's plan. It will go down as a major win for me.

Jesus resisted the offer and reminded the devil of the written Word which commanded worship of the Lord God, serving Him only (Matthew 4:9-10). Jesus set the example for us to follow in overcoming the evil one's temptation. Jesus sent a direct message to His followers—even in your weakest moment, depend on the Word to overcome evil and the devil's ploys. The Word was effective in upholding a shield to prevent the enemy from gaining ground and executing his plan.

Hebrews 12:2 offers the answer to guarding our eyes against a wretched lustful snare. We establish safeguards by "fixing our eyes on Jesus, the author and perfecter of faith".

You will never grow tired or weary from looking unto Jesus. Stay focused.

Adam and Eve did not fully comprehend the far-reaching consequences that would follow their mindless, fleshly pursuit. After the first bite, Adam and Eve experienced the effects of sin by recognizing their nakedness. Nakedness was never an issue prior to the act of disobedience. Instantly, the mindset shifted from spiritual awareness to the physical.

The accompanying shadow with sin was shame. In the time it took to eat one bite, Adam and Eve went from openness and purity to hiding and concealing. Again operating from natural instincts, Adam and Eve benefitted from creation in an attempt to address the nakedness. First, the fig leaves intended to keep the tree healthy and aid in producing fruit were used for a covering. Next, the intellect given as a gift from God was used in concocting a scheme to remedy the shame. And lastly, man who was created wholly for God realigned his allegiance, his heart, by listening and following a different voice.

All of these actions revealed perversions by taking what was meant for good and misusing for selfish gain. Conveniently after the first bite was taken, the snake went silent, and Adam and Eve were left on their own to figure things out. An effective practice utilized against us presently. He mastered making false promises to lead us his way and then abandoned us unexpectedly leaving us to figure out how we ended up in such trouble.

Satan accomplished the mission as soon as the attention was diverted away from God. Was he in shock and speechless that his craftiness actually worked with Adam and Eve? Was he marveling over the manipulation created by his hand? From the Bible we know that Adam and Eve were not celebrating with him. Their sin and shame sent them into hiding from God.

This was the first attempt to separate physically from God due to shame. Prior to Satan entering the Garden, Adam and Eve enjoyed open exchanges, intimacy, and fellowship with God. The introduction of sin created a chasm in which man was no longer privileged with free access. Adam and Eve underestimated or failed to revere the demands of a holy God upon His creation.

God will not compromise His holiness even if it means sacrificing the relationship between man and Himself.

God and man possess two distinct natures that separate the two from co-existing without special provision. Habakkuk described God's holiness as eyes "too pure to approve evil, and You cannot look on wickedness with favor" (1:13).

God made provision to reconcile the relationship with man through a promised Savior, the seed of the woman in Genesis 3:15.

According to this verse, Adam and Eve were to anticipate from their descendant one who would deliver a crushing defeat to the seed of the enemy. Jesus Christ provided an overwhelming crushing blow by overcoming the enemy with His resurrection from the dead.

Satan, the author of death, was unable to sustain his power over Jesus. And as believers in Jesus Christ, the Victor, we are not bound in death either, as we will one day experience the same resurrection power (1 Corinthians 15:20).

One of Jesus' roles in our lives is to provide a way for us to have access to God.

> *"I am the way, and the truth, and the life; no one comes to the Father but through Me."*
>
> *John 14:6*

We need Jesus to enjoy a relationship similar to Adam and Eve in the Garden. Through Jesus, we gain greater insight into God the Father, His holiness and righteousness. God's holiness and expectations for His creation have not changed in this evolving world. In our natural state, we will never be pure enough to meet God's holy standards. We need Jesus to bridge the gap with His righteousness and fulfill the requirements on our behalf in order to be united with God, our Father. Otherwise, Peter says we will be "continually straying like sheep, but now you have returned to the Shepherd and Guardian of your souls" (1 Peter 2:25).

When the Father looks upon the believer, He doesn't see our self-righteousness and feeble attempts to provide for ourselves. God sees His Son's righteousness shining on our behalf.

God sees the believer as one who identifies with His obedient Son who made many righteous by serving as the sacrifice and taking on the sin of many (Romans 5:19).

> *"For this reason also, God highly exalted Him, and bestowed on Him the name which is above every name, so that at the name of Jesus every knee will bow, of those who are in heaven and on earth and under the earth and that every tongue will confess that Jesus Christ is Lord, to the glory of God the Father."*
>
> *Philippians 2:9-11*

Jesus finalizes His earthly mission on the cross when He uttered the words, "It is finished" (John 19:30). Jesus promises to return us to the worshipful conditions that existed in the Garden of Eden, uninterrupted fellowship with our Father. Until that time occurs, we demonstrate our faithfulness by putting on the mind of Christ.

A life hidden in Christ exchanges shame for security. Since we continue to endure the consequences of Adam and Eve's actions, we cling to hope. Until the appropriate time, we will endure setbacks and disappointments, but remain mindful of God's promises even in our failures.

> *Set your minds on the things above, not on the things that are on earth. For you have died and your life is hidden with Christ in God.*
>
> *Colossians 3:2-3*

Contemplation Corner

1. How are you practicing mindfulness in your spiritual life today? If this is not a current practice, how do you plan to start implementing it?

2. What does it mean to you to put on the mind of Christ? Read Colossians 3 for more insight.

3. What lie has the evil one been successful in whispering to you?

4. Is there any shame or guilt that you would like to be free of today?

5. Why is it important to you to practice mindfulness in Christ? How will this practice make a difference for you? Your family? Your co-workers?

6. What is holding you back from getting started in practicing mindfulness or expressing a desire to do so?

Chapter 3
Be Curious

Read: John 3:1-3; 19:38-40

> *Now there was a man of the Pharisees, named Nicodemus, a ruler of the Jews; this man came to Jesus by night and said to Him, "Rabbi, we know that You have come from God as a teacher; for no one can do these signs that You do unless God is with him." Jesus answered and said to him, "Truly, truly, I say to you, unless one is born again he cannot see the kingdom of God."*
> John 3:1-3

A nosy neighbor who peers into our backyard constantly may be overbearing at times. But one thing we cannot find fault with is her curiosity. Curiosity will cause us to leave our comforts and explore the unknown in search of an awaiting answer.

We can thank the curious minds for the conveniences we enjoy today. An irreplaceable invention, the cell phone, began with a person of a curious nature. One day, a persistent thought challenged an innovative mindset, and a dream was birthed out of a curious pursuit.

Surely along the way there was resistance. There were those who preferred the status quo and found the land line sufficient to meet communicative needs. If you can reach 9-1-1, what more does one really need? Who knew that constant communication via talking and texting offered as much appeal as drive-thru coffee shops? Those swept along by curiosity do not permit the naysayers the opportunity to squash their fervor.

Curiosity is the energy that keeps us moving forward through thrashing waves of data until we reach a satisfying answer. One question leads to another and voila a cell phone in the hands of over 60% of the world's population. Billions say yes to this device and incorporate it into their lifestyles. Alexander Graham Bell would consider the far-reaching scope of his initial idea to be a true head-scratcher. And all this progress can be traced back to curiosity which has the power to fan an ember into a massive explosion.

Nicodemus, the Curious Seeker

The Bible introduces Nicodemus whom most will agree had a curious nature. Nicodemus was an educated man of power and position. His education provided him with knowledge and proper handling of the Scripture. As a trustworthy servant, he studied and taught responsibly. He was a Pharisee who believed that one day the Messiah would provide national deliverance for his people. Nicodemus, as a ruler of the Jews, experienced respect from his fellow man for all the time and efforts he poured into knowing God. He was a man of elevated status who enjoyed acquiring knowledge and sharing with genuine and sincere motivations. Nicodemus was admired for his faithfulness and commitment. He represented the true embodiment of a faithful teacher.

Jesus, the all-wise and all-knowing God, knew Nicodemus intimately prior to making his in-person acquaintance. Before deciding to make a move to approach Jesus, Nicodemus observed Jesus in action, listened to rumors and then planned an encounter. His information gathering led him to conclude that Jesus was a teacher sent from God. The signs were too significant to attribute to a mere man void of supernatural power and strength. These signs captured the attention of those burdened with illnesses, hunger, or other life circumstances.

Few were perturbed by the Jews' ongoing concerns. Certainly, there were by far more pressing issues for the Roman rulers such as increasing domineering power and maintaining authority. Until Jesus arrived on the scene, some Jews lived in oppressive misery and bore their wounds wearily. Jesus performed signs to address the persistent hopelessness. The miracles were precise and tailored-made to fit the individual's specific need. There was no doubt that God intervened in man's earthly affairs demonstrating concern and compassion for His creation.

The signs carried a compelling message which pointed to God for the recipient(s) or observers to believe in Him. Each sign was as if an archer pulled back a bow, aimed at the target and released in order to point the attention to God and away from distractions and self.

People were drawn to Jesus for various reasons. The miraculous signs were effective for some and not so for others. In Nicodemus's case, the signs were captivating and thought-provoking enough for him to instigate a personal investigation. His next step was an in-person visit, garnering undivided attention to get all his questions answered.

Nicodemus devised a plan in which he was assured no crowds and minimal distractions. Birthed out of curiosity was a craving to have Jesus all to himself. A fixated mind on God and eyes to recognize supernatural acts were motivations to fuel Nicodemus onward. He was driven to know the rest of the story and confirm his assessment based on observations.

Curiosity Lurking in Dark Places

The first step in Nicodemus's plan was selecting the ideal time. He chose a time that guaranteed quiet, minimal distractions, and availability. Jesus was gaining popularity as the word began to spread throughout communities. The needs were plentiful. Jesus forged a reputation shaped by His willingness to help and compassion for the people. He even made time for the children to come. Nicodemus was careful not to interfere with Jesus' day to day concerns. Nicodemus, a studious man of ideas and people, chose the night to approach Jesus.

Nicodemus approaching Jesus in darkness presents a classic contrast. In a dark hour of the night, Nicodemus who is walking in darkness (literally and, soon to be discovered, spiritually as well as mentally) seeks the source of light to gain insight and understanding.

Jesus says, "I have come as Light into the world, so that everyone who believes in Me will not remain in darkness" (Jn 12:46).

Darkness appears to be comforting and inviting while luring into a den of deceit. The mission is to cover the truth and block out the possibility of seeing an alternative way.

Darkness wants us to believe there is no way out.

We are required to figure things out for ourselves permanently. There is no other savior. We have to save ourselves.

A lifestyle indwelt in darkness depends on craftiness in order to claw up to manmade success. A commitment to self-serving plans and strategies which rewards and shapes your values is the price to pay for admission into this life-robbing abyss.

Does this sound like Satan in the garden? Once Adam and Eve succumbed to Satan's suggestion, the transition from light to darkness was instantaneous.

Unless we make an intentional decision to believe in Jesus Christ, we remain surrounded by darkness in a lost state. The longer we prefer spending idle time in darkness, the further we drift away from the shoreline where light resides.

What does the light provide? Clarity. When I flip a switch, a dark room becomes orderly, and I can proceed with confidence. Jesus serves the exact same role in our lives. Once we enter the light, we experience a veil lifting and a magnetic pull to follow Christ. We proceed with assurance and certainty not in our ability, but in Christ alone.

Romans 8 tells us that God predestined us to "*become* conformed to the image of His Son" (29). Clarity is the act of moment by moment conforming to

Christ which takes place in the light only. It is a high calling to desire to look like, behave like, speak like, touch like, and love like Jesus Christ. In doing so, we starve an indwelt nature that wants to do the exact opposite.

Romans 8:37, "But in all these things we overwhelmingly conquer through Him who loved us". The Greek word for overwhelmingly conquer is hypernikomen. Hyper does not mean a tiny smidgen. On the contrary, hyper indicates to prevail mightily, above and beyond.

Our English word, nike, derives from a Greek mythological goddess who represents victory. The name means to conquer, overcome, and prevail. Nike, the well-known sports brand, expresses this grand victory with a logo commonly referred to as the Swoosh. The Swoosh is the visual and audible symbol that highlights the brand as capable of delivering prevailing results, movement, and power to its buyers. With this understanding, the tag line – Just Do It – deems to be most appropriate. With the assurance of grand victories, the Nike consumer is without excuse for going forth in accomplishing goals. Coupling the above and beyond results with grand victories, the buyer receives the promise to experience above and beyond performance during athletic pursuits.

These victories cannot be accomplished in darkness

while alone in our own strength and power. The Nike brand highlights this benefit while marketing its products as the partnering victor. Swoosh. For the believer, overwhelming conquering occurs in the light through Jesus Christ, the source of light.

Nicodemus arrives in a darkened state, however, his demeanor at departure remains unclear. The Bible provides no details outlining Nicodemus's curiosity after his meeting. Evidence supports that Jesus makes an impactful imprint on Nicodemus that continues even after the encounter.

Later, Nicodemus accompanies Joseph of Arimathea, a secret disciple, in John 19:38-40. Joseph and Nicodemus prepare a proper burial for Jesus. Clues are scarce whether Nicodemus lives, as Joseph, in secrecy fearing scrutiny and ostracism from unbelieving Jews. John concludes Nicodemus's story with him contributing a mixture of myrrh and aloes, roughly a hundred pounds. Joseph and Nicodemus assume responsibility for the body, bind it in linen wrappings with the spices, and place it in a new tomb.

Donating a hundred pounds of spices for an acquaintance's burial is not an insignificant contribution. Nicodemus closes his encounter with the Messiah by demonstrating honor and respect to Jesus out of his own wealth with a generous contribution. Generosity is a common trait that is typically shared by believers who are grateful for the opportunity to be in the presence of Light. Giving from your resources is a supernatural response to the gift that Jesus gave freely.

Curiosity in the Light

Jesus wasted no time with arbitrary pleasantries and futile introductions. Clearly, a mutual recognition was in play. Nicodemus learned about Jesus from afar. Jesus was intimately familiar with Nicodemus via omniscience. At this point, Nicodemus's curious nature yielded dividends with an in-person meeting with Jesus Christ.

The obligation that accompanied this opportunity was responsibility. Nicodemus was obligated to handle his newly acquired information carefully as well as respond responsibly.

> An encounter with Christ requires a choice to be made.

An encounter with Christ requires a choice to be made. An unresponsive response is a choice to ignore divine intervention.

Surrendering to Christ serves as a safeguard against Satan's wanderings and manipulations. "and do not give the devil an opportunity" (Ephesians 4:27). Becoming more like Christ may be an intrinsic desire, but putting in the work, foregoing self, creates tension as the spirit and flesh meet face to face, staring down one another defiantly. Neither willing to bow out gracefully.

Nicodemus demonstrates this principle beautifully as he engages in an internal struggle to reconcile Jesus' words with his present understanding.

I recall a time in which I perceived God asking me to trust Him with my children. The spirit was willing to do whatever pleased God, but the flesh? Not so amenable. I was a stay-at-home mom who chose to set aside my career and spend time with my children. I managed our home and children just like the projects that had come across my desk when I had been in the work force. (The only exceptions were the hugs and kisses that smothered my kids. Those were not so much my work projects.)

Until one day, I sensed God intervening into our daily affairs by asking me to return my children to Him. Of all the things to ask for, my joy, my heart, my love and not least of all my sweet peas.

In my mind, I was more than capable of protecting and caring for them. I knew the future that I had for my children—top notch education, prominence, etc. As long as looked the other way and ignored God's request, I was tossed around in personal turmoil. The request seemed too much for anyone to ask of a mother. One day, unable to carry on in my own created dysfunction, I gave up the struggle. The struggle was one-sided anyway since God was quite content to wait for me to return to my good mind. The release allowed me to enjoy my children while simultaneously giving me a peace of mind again.

Deep down I believed that I was doing what was best for my children. On the contrary, I chose a path certain to lead to hurt for my children as well as myself, because I was picking and choosing parts of God that suited me. Honestly speaking, I was beginning to erect a kingdom that attempted to rival God.

What was wrong with encouraging each child to reach for the highest aspiration? Nothing, but I was the one deciding the highest point and choosing paths for each child without consulting God for His plan. With good intentions in tow, I had stepped into the creator's rolc.

The Word is clear, "You shall have no other god before me (Deuteronomy 5:7). I realized that we could not both be God. I surrendered.

Today, my children are free to be whomever God created them to be. And witnessing their evolution as well as mine brings immeasurable joy. God cares too much for my children, His children, to allow my ignorance to interfere with His loving plan. In His infinite wisdom, He foresaw the enemy's visit to my children, carrying an enticing candy basket filled with empty promises and temptations. The only way for children to choose not to yield to temptation is by starting to build their own trusting relationship with God and understanding that His love is superior to anything the world has to offer.

God possesses an exponentially better plan for my children and for me as a mother.

Curiosity in Ignorance

Continuing in the vein of sweeping away ignorance, Jesus was laser-focused on Nicodemus's gaping hole in his spiritual understanding and knowledge. As Nicodemus desired to meet with Jesus, the same was true of Jesus as He had crucial information to share. Jesus opted to address the glaring urgent matter head on without any hesitation. Nicodemus was oblivious to any sense of urgency. A casual stimulating exchange was probably enough to satisfy the man, a chat with a fellow teacher. Nicodemus was not proclaiming Jesus to be the Messiah, so maybe he saw Him as a great guy who loved God just like himself.

Nicodemus concluded that Jesus was sent from God accurately. This assessment left little room for him to wiggle out of the meeting once he heard something that did not mesh well with his understanding. Yet, his conclusion that Jesus was sent from God as a teacher was only partial truth in summarizing Jesus in His totality. A partially accurate judgment lowered the expectations for this impending meeting.

What did Nicodemus really hope to gain from meeting with Jesus? More knowledge to possess with hopes to become a better teacher or ruler? Possibly. With cracks in his understanding, Nicodemus approached Jesus man-to-man with a common love for God. The lack of worship and reverence were absolute indicators that Nicodemus approached Jesus as another man.

In the presence of God, man worships instantaneously and instinctively. Nicodemus was clueless as to what was about to transpire in this interaction. Jesus' stunning magnificence will play topsy turvy with Nicodemus's limited knowledge, prestige, position, and power. In other words, Jesus was not impressed with man's acuity when it lacked a proper foundation in God's Word. Jesus was unrelenting in His mission to help others understand God and His will for their lives. The stage was set for Nicodemus to experience an upheaval that would be uncomfortable and challenging for him to accept.

Maybe you can relate to Nicodemus's topsy turvy experience. In your mind, you are confident in the direction in which you are pursuing. And without any warnings whatsoever, you find yourself grasping to get a grip on reality. Or you get this feeling in the pit of your stomach that something is just not quite right.

A friend of mine arrived at the testing center prepared to take the MCAT, the next logical step to fulfill a dream of becoming a doctor. Upon arrival, he was met with an overwhelming sensation to be somewhere else, on the mission field. Unable to silence the persistent voices that were incessant in getting his attention, he left the testing center and enrolled in seminary. Upon graduating, he and his wife relocated to the mission field in Haiti. A place described as antithetical to the comforts of a doctor's lifestyle. Their lives are plagued by earthquakes, poverty, and political unrest and yet completely fulfilling. If you asked them to return to the states, the answer would be no.

God is an expert at placing His people exactly where He wants in His timing.

They are not ready to transfer the work that they love to the next ones called to labor. Their hearts are committed to improving the lives of the less fortunate by providing hands-on basic living staples and biblical knowledge.

Sometimes it is difficult to walk away from dreams and plans. Holding on becomes reality and at that point, there will likely be struggles and tensions while the choices are made to align in agreement with God on His purpose. The key is to continue making choices and trusting God.

God is an expert at placing His people exactly where He wants in His timing.

Through Moses, God spoke to Pharaoh and revealed His purpose. "But, indeed, for this reason I have allowed you to remain, in order to show you My power and in order to proclaim My name through all the earth" (Exodus 9:16). If God chose purpose in the pagan, how much more so in the child who belongs to Him? Ultimate purpose in any life that belongs to God is to always proclaim God's name and make Him known throughout the extent of your influence.

Before exploring Nicodemus's interaction, let us pause and consider a different way to approach matters out of curiosity. The best way to satisfy curiosity is to remain open and receptive without preconceived notions. Nicodemus's observations led him to conclude that Jesus was a teacher sent from God based on His observed works. But as a reader you get the sense that his thoughts did not reach further than considering Jesus as only a man. Nicodemus seemed to be closed-minded to the possibility of Jesus being more than mere human. The words from the prophets describing the future Messiah were not considered. Interestingly, Jesus did not disclose to Nicodemus His status of being God present in flesh. "And the Word became flesh and dwelt among us" (John 1:14a).

Jesus interacted with Nicodemus as with others by beginning the conversation at his personal point of need. Nicodemus was not ready to receive that Jesus was the long-awaited Messiah. So, Jesus focused on the knowledge that was necessary at that moment without revealing the complete story in one setting. Nicodemus's unsuspecting needs were what he prized the most, understanding and knowledge.

A good student always assumes that the teacher's time is precious. Such opportunity must not be wasted. The idea is for the seeker to know nothing, remaining in a position to examine the newly acquired knowledge from an objective perspective prior to deciding whether to accept or reject.

A tennis coach, Jorge Fernandez employs a similar strategy in discovering and growing in knowledge. "The art of being a great coach is understanding that you know nothing," Jorge told The Globe and Mail. "And when you know nothing, all you do is get hungry to find out." Jorge discovered that successful strategies were obtained by being open to learning through curiosity.

Curiosity in the Kingdom

Nicodemus made the first move in opening the discussion with Jesus. He did not get very far as Jesus was short on time to entertain flattery. Too much was at stake. In Jesus' presence was a teacher whom people entrusted to deliver principles and truths accurately. The imminent danger of teaching without understanding was the potential to lead others astray with ensuing devastating consequences. Nicodemus shared that the signs that Jesus had performed captured his attention. Nicodemus stated that he knew Jesus was from God indicating that Nicodemus was operating under the assumption that he knew God also. So the teacher identified Jesus as a person from God based on His works and Nicodemus's own personal knowledge.

In other words, You are from God because I know God and matters pertaining to God.

Jesus' next words were drop-the-mic worthy. In so many words, if you know God then why are you not familiar with the things of God such as His kingdom?

> *Truly, truly, I say to you, unless one is born again he cannot see the kingdom of God.*
>
> *John 3:3*

Nicodemus as a ruler and teacher presumed that he

held the road map to the kingdom of God. In his mind, he not only saw the kingdom, but he was pointing others to see God's kingdom as well. His days were spent studying and teaching topics relating to God.

Astonishing were the words from Jesus. Nicodemus grappled with them, but he couldn't change his mind and declare that he'd made a mistake by believing the Rabbi was from God. He'd already stated his belief that Jesus was from God. Nicodemus was committed to this divine appointment and had to remain, as if trapped by quicksand, unable to back away slowly. Nicodemus was staring down truth, eye-to-eye literally.

With a bold opening statement, Jesus informed Nicodemus that he was not close enough to even see the kingdom. Now the darkened backdrop is perfect as Nicodemus needed a space without distractions to process this preposterous declaration.

Certainly from all his studies, Nicodemus was intimately aware of God and His kingdom, or so he thought. Whatever Nicodemus was missing in his understanding and instructions represented something of tremendous value, a grave oversight.

Jesus used simple words like being born again. The words were simple but the meaning was far from it. Jesus brought to life the words that John wrote in 1:12-13, "But as many as received Him, to them He gave the right to become children of God, even to those who believe in His name, who were born, not of blood nor of the will of the flesh nor of the will of man, but of God." Jesus was referring to a spiritual birth, a righteous renewal process between God and the individual. Nicodemus, fixated on the present natural reality, was unable to interpret the significance of these words, born of the will of God. Mystery shrouded this humanly speaking second birth. The physical sight has limitations that preclude from understanding spiritual meaning and applications. Principles such as this led Paul to instruct the Corinthians to "walk by faith not by sight" (2 Corinthians 5:7).

In the natural world, parents decide to participate in the birthing process. Spiritually, God chooses your birth before forming you as an embryo in your mother's womb. This is a classic difference between natural and spiritual perspectives.

The spiritual implications are far more reaching than the natural. Jesus' words challenged Nicodemus to elevate his thinking beyond a literal, physical, earthly translation. Nicodemus's response indicated an intense internal struggle. "How can these things be?" (John 3:9). And yet, Jesus remains unphased by the perplexity surrounding His stated position. With clear, concise, and unchanging words, Jesus commits to His stance without wavering - "You must be born again" (John 3:7).

Nicodemus took pride in his natural birth and heritage. He was born with a lineage to Abraham into a race of a chosen people. God spoke to Abraham and said, And in you all the families of the earth will be blessed (Gen 12:3b). Meaning not just Abraham and his descendants, but an open-ended invitation for all people. Nicodemus's sense of security resided in his people, traditions, and the prophets to shape his kingdom vision. Somehow, his proud identity with the natural and physical descent intercepted and clouded his kingdom perception. The kingdom was not a place for Jews to enter by carrying a natural birthright card.

You must be born again.

This truth serves as an applicable reminder for us today. Growing up in a home with Christian parents is not a ticket for entrance into the kingdom. A holy and righteous birthing process is open to anyone willing to accept the right to become a child of God. The key word is *accept*. Entrance into the kingdom is predicated upon belief.

Belief in whom? Belief in the Son who maintains sole authority for admission.

Nicodemus responded to Jesus' declaration out of physical sight, "how can a man be born when he is old? He cannot enter a second time into his mother's womb and be born, can he?" (John 3:4). Here again,

Nicodemus's words were completely focused on the natural and the physical. His words reflected upon natural experiences such as his mother's womb, a man, the birth canal. Nicodemus revealed his ignorance and confusion when he asked.

Man cannot reenter and recreate a different birthing experience worthy of the kingdom. Once upon a time, a mother's womb provided warmth, protection, and security for nine months. Eventually, the womb reached its limitations and expectations. The baby exited the womb through expulsion by pushing during contractions. The precious and delicate womb was created for a forty-week gestation period with a specific function to house life, but not eternally. No matter how much I longed to protect my firstborn and provide him with security, nine pounds were the full extent for my womb. Reaching that point, I was grateful for his introduction into the world and the relief for my body.

In contrast, God includes no restraints or painful contractions with His invitation to be born again of His will. The born-again spiritual experience is for each individual to participate freely. A standing invitation for this spiritual encounter remains open for everyone throughout a lifetime.

Whatever man has to offer always entails limitations and insufficiencies. Man is incapable of performing enough works on his own behalf to satisfy a holy God, establish security or gain entrance into the everlasting kingdom. This entrance into the kingdom will not be dependent upon man and his efforts, incomplete knowledge or earthly family members.

> "For all have sinned and fall short of the glory of *God."*
>
> *Romans 3:23*

All fall short except one, Jesus Christ. Jesus Christ is the only one qualified to deliver into the kingdom. Nicodemus's responses indicate this pertinent missing information.

> *"Truly, truly, I say to you, unless one is born of water and the Spirit he cannot enter in the kingdom of God. That which is born of the flesh is flesh, and which is born of the Spirit is spirit."*
>
> *John 3:5-6*

> *"For the flesh sets its desire against the Spirit, and the Spirit against the flesh; for these are in opposition to one another, so that you may not do the things that you please."*
>
> *Galatians 5:17*

The flesh has an affinity to entertain "immorality, impurity, sensuality, idolatry, sorcery, enmities, strife, jealousy, outbursts of anger, disputes, dissensions, factions, envying, drunkenness, carousing, and things like these . . ." (Galatians 5:19-21). The kingdom makes no accommodations for the flesh. The natural physical birth resides outside the spiritual realm.

The kingdom of God ostracizes any manifestations that contradict holiness. *You must be born again* sets a clear intention that a spiritual renewal is necessary to crucify the flesh and replace it with characteristics that resemble Jesus, gladly exchanging the fleshly desires for the Spirit's outpouring of "love, joy, peace, patience, kindness, goodness, faithfulness, gentleness, self-control . . ." (Gen 5:22).

The kingdom belongs to God—His realm and jurisdiction. Since the kingdom belongs to God, He has the sovereign authority to establish the standards for entrance. Perfect holiness and righteousness belong to Jesus, the faithful Son. Jesus is the only one qualified to enter the kingdom outright without any special provisions.

Nicodemus had an important decision to make regarding whether to accept Jesus. Before updating his teaching manual, he first had to subject himself to becoming a student of Jesus and not a peer or fellow teacher. Today, God remains unimpressed by who we know, how much we know, or how much work we do, even on His behalf. None of these things will gain access into His kingdom. God directs His children to the spiritual realm. And in this realm, He examines the heart searching for love for Him and His Son.

> *For He whom God has sent speaks the words of God; for He gives the Spirit without measure. The Father loves the Son and has given all things into His hand. He who believes in the Son has eternal life . . .*
>
> *John 3:34-36*

Anyone desiring access to the kingdom of God must trust the Spirit to lead to the Son. No one can enter or see the kingdom of God without God's Son.

How did Nicodemus land a meeting with Jesus Christ? Curiosity. Curiosity fuels momentum to press forward while acquiring, dismissing, and accumulating knowledge along the way. Even when the trail leads to the most perplexing data, it will propel someone to wrestle through it, draw conclusions, and move forward. This movement rests within the power of the Holy Spirit to reveal God in our lives.

The risk paid off royally for Nicodemus.

Being curious requires taking a risk to experience the reward. We should be curious about Christ who promises eternal rewards for believers

> *O, God, You are my God; I shall seek You earnestly; My soul thirst for You, my flesh yearns for You, in a dry*

and weary land where there is no water.

Psalm 63:1

Contemplation Corner:

1. Are you as meticulous as Nicodemus in planning a time to meet with Jesus?

2. What is your thought process once you discover teachings in the Bible that are contrary to your beliefs and understanding?

3. Jesus permitted Nicodemus ample time to ask his questions. Are you comfortable in bringing your questions before Jesus?

4. What steps do you take to ensure that you do not impose your ideas on God?

5. What do you love about Nicodemus?

6. What do you love about Jesus based on his interaction with Nicodemus?

7. Write about your born-again experience.

8. If you have not encountered a born-again experience, will you profess your belief and faith in Jesus Christ at this very moment?

Chapter 4
Be Aware

Read Matthew 16:21-23

> *But He turned and said to Peter, "Get behind Me, Satan! You are a stumbling block to Me; for you are not setting your mind on God's interests, but man's."*
>
> *Matthew 16:23.*

Awareness is one of those attributes that will get pushed aside and buried under busyness if not intentionally and actively monitored. An aware person maintains a keen sense of surroundings through perception and seeks continuous understanding.

Sleepwalkers personify the opposite demeanor. Fascinating to watch, sleepwalkers appear to be alert with open eyes and making decisions. Upon further observation, you soon realize that something is not quite right. Mentally, a sleepwalker's mind is resting in bed while the body prowls on a mission. The mind and body are not in sync during a sleepwalking exercise.

My daughter was startled awake during the middle of the night. My son, an occasional sleepwalker, had gone to the restroom. All was going well until he missed the cues to return to his bedroom opting for the first available bedroom door. When he opened the door, his light-sleeping sister called his name. Her voice registered *wrong door* in his mind. A slight turn had him resting in his bed again soundly. The next day, we enjoyed hearing the story relayed by our daughter. Our son was completely unaware of his nighttime wanderings, and denied the occurrence ever took place. Since he was sleepwalking, his denial carried very little weight. I trusted the sister's detailed report and blamed it on his dad for contributing suspicious genes.

As a life coach, I have many clients faced with important and time-sensitive matters. The trouble is, some of them tend to *sleepwalk* through these crucial times and decisions. In some sessions, we're set to discuss something totally different, but stumble over an issue that hides away in the corner avoiding attention, I attempt to shine light in that direction. Typically, an initial response from the client supports maintaining status quo. It is like watching a deer in headlights frozen in thought and disposition. A thoughtful discussion coerces the issue to the forefront for the next active step toward resolution. It is a rewarding experience to help another sweep away cobwebs and regain healthy mental space for increased awareness to occupy.

Awareness Requires Full Understanding

Sleepwalkers are unaware of their situations. In their unconscious state, they have limited perceptions and understanding.

Peter showed some of the same as he lacked awareness in his encounter with Jesus. Peter demonstrated his difficulty in processing and managing truth shared by Jesus. The words spoken by Jesus misaligned with Peter's vision. Unbeknownst to Peter, his response indicated a desire for Jesus to rewrite truth to meet his distorted perception.

Jesus communicated to His disciples who were trusted confidants and members of the inner circle, a truth that was challenging to understand. The disciples struggled with what to do with Jesus. Those who made decisions to leave families, professions, stability in exchange for a commitment to Jesus Christ second guessed. The risks were worth the potential rewards, but this announcement cast unanticipated doubt. Jesus introduced an earth-shattering plan that included deliberate suffering. He fixated on the route to Jerusalem, a place that represented death, the end. While operating under a lack of awareness, the disciples failed to recognize that Jesus never intended to leave them vulnerable and hopeless.

The Scripture recorded key words, "Jesus began to show His disciples . . ." (Matthew 16:21). Jesus began to teach His disciples to prepare them for what lay ahead. Unawareness felt like abandonment in this moment. The moment was nothing short of love. At no time, did Jesus ever consider abandoning His followers. "I am the good shepherd, and I know My own and My own know Me, even as the Father knows Me and I know the Father; and I lay down My life for the sheep" (John 10:14-15). The words spoken in assurance with authority intended to comfort and relieve anxiety regarding the future. However, the words delivered to an audience without awareness accomplished the opposite impact. Fear set in for the listeners.

Fear is a natural outcome of a lack of awareness or complete understanding especially when the present appears uncertain. In such a case, fear can be used as an advantage to work in our favor as a prompter. Oftentimes, we experience physical signs whenever fear is present. The moment I received the unwanted results from my EKG, my gut was the first to respond. Then, my mind followed with constant potential negative outcomes. The doctor remained focused on her mission to provide excellent

> *Awareness is assessing the situation and moving forward with the information on hand.*

medical care with more testing. I was on the brink of accepting an invitation to swim with sharks in the sea of unawareness. Soon I realized the counter productivity and unnecessity in following these poisoned thought trails.

Awareness is assessing the situation and moving forward with the information on hand. The doctor sought more information as nothing was conclusive without further tests. That one revealed a false read but identified another minor concern requiring future monitoring. All in all the tests worked in my favor and I felt incredibly blessed after the results. If left untamed, unawareness places you at a disadvantage and prompts fear-based thinking.

Jesus who loved the disciples had no desires to keep them unaware. He shared His plan with them to shut the door on actions driven by fear. Just as the door handle was meeting the latch, Peter spoke. Too late. Fear slithered in by a fractioned second. The announcement intended to bring awareness rocked their world. So much so that Peter immersed in his dreams and ideology, rebuked Jesus for speaking absurdity. Fear caused Peter to forget the previous healings, teachings, and miracles. Peter assumed a tone that reprimanded Jesus for sharing His plan. "God forbid it, Lord! This shall never happen to You" (Matthew 16:22).

Before we start wagging the finger of shame at Peter, let us examine our hearts and actions. How easily do we displace Jesus as God and reduce His status equal to or less than ours? The Scripture captures a raw moment with Peter that is relatable.

Peter's words echo our sentiments when we encounter contradictions to our plans. He presents a precise reaction to truth that passes through a selfish nature.

My first response in such a situation is to figure out and express how my wellbeing will fare in this revelatory truth. 'What about me?'

Moments when we find ourselves differing from Jesus Christ are priceless in exposing our identity.

Somehow, we revert to our two-year-old nature that wants to throw a tantrum when we don't get our way. We never really outgrow it. We don't fall down in the middle of the store, kick and scream for attention. Instead, we employ more sophisticated tactics, using our words to coerce, manipulate and persuade others to agree with us. We control situations and people for our greater good and satisfaction.

Moments when we find ourselves differing from Jesus Christ are priceless in exposing our identity. These moments lay bare the stuff that serves as obstacles in our relationships with Jesus. As our love, respect and admiration increase for Jesus, we become more adamant about addressing offensive intruders that aim to divide and separate us from truth.

Growing in maturity in Christ means we don't always have to understand or agree with the godly plan. However, we must be aware that God's plan is by far greater than anything conceivable by man. In practicality, this stance releases us from engaging in arguments for the sake of winning. We are free to experience life from a perspective that does not serve to protect us at all costs. As parents who live this truth, we enjoy our children and do not overprotect or micromanage their lives. We simply become free to trust God and His plan to work on behalf of those whom He loves more than we are capable of loving.

Although it may be difficult to accept the differences in my plans versus God's plans, the efforts to conform to Jesus are worthwhile. As followers of Jesus, we crave lessons that bring clarity to the colored sinful lens in which we view everything. After repeated damaging encounters with contradictory godly viewpoints, we chip away at the lies accepted as truths. We redirect our minds to think upon God's interests and decrease the stake in our own agenda. This imparts a clear valuation of godly awareness.

Jesus teaches us this principle when He prays in the Garden of Gethsemane, "yet not My will, but Yours be done" (Luke 22:42). And again, in the Lord's prayer, "Your kingdom come. Your will be done, On earth as it is in heaven" (Matthew 6:10).

It is never a battle of my will versus God's will for that conflict was won on Calvary. God possesses immeasurable power so He does not consider us a formidable foe to meet on the battlefield. He sees me as someone who is helpless and needs Him desperately. He holds the power over life and death. The one-sided struggle is within me to accept God's will to be like His Son and walk with Him daily.

God waits patiently for us to surrender to His love, grace and mercy.

> *Therefore the Lord longs to be gracious to you, and therefore He waits on high to have compassion on you. For the Lord is a God of justice; how blessed are all those who long for Him.*
>
> *Isaiah 30:18*

Oftentimes, we perceive God as a restrictive, judgmental, out-to-catch-me-to-inflict-punishment type. A disciplinarian. This perception challenges John 3:16, "For God so loved the world, that He gave His only begotten Son, that whoever believes in Him shall not perish, but have eternal life".

If God wants to catch me in the act of wrongdoing, I am so grateful to be caught by such loving and protective hands. God's discipline, correcting my behavior to conform to His desire, teaches me the meaning and value of a life worthy of my calling. Without a true depiction of God based on His Word, my lack of understanding leads to living contrary to God's principles and in bondage totally unaware of the misalignment with God's interests.

Humanly speaking, Peter's words are relatable to those wanting an alternative outcome. Peter says aloud what others are thinking. "This shall never happen to You" (Matthew 16:22). In an earlier verse, Peter declares Jesus as "the Christ, the Son of the living God" (Matthew 16:16). He experiences a divine interaction by receiving this revelation directly from the Father who is in heaven (Matthew 16:17). It is a mountain-top, glorious moment in which Peter aligns in thought and words with God's heavenly plan. He exuberates awareness at its core. He also illustrates that awareness requires work. As quickly as he rejoices in his awareness, he falls into a state of unawareness by disagreeing with God adamantly.

Peter acts upon his impulse and tries to thrust his opinion upon Jesus with forceful intonations. The mind-shift occurs as soon as the plan runs congruent to Peter. He responds with disdain. According to Peter, the plan must unfold as he envisions. Which parts of the plan are offensive to Peter? Maybe he becomes unsettled with the part in which Jesus predicts His suffering leading to death. The Person whom Peter sees as hope will soon be inaccessible to him. How disappointing for the man in that as soon as he recognizes the Christ, he will utter goodbye in a foreseeable near future. Peter is unable to recognize any benefits for himself or his people from a dead Christ. Certainly, he expects his decision to join Jesus, separating from family and a productive fishing career, to yield benefits greater than death in Jerusalem. Part of what troubles him has to do with the 'what about me syndrome'. Peter finds himself in a quandary. The plan according to his understanding includes no special accommodations for his goals and aspirations. This conclusion is enough for Peter to request Jesus to rethink the heavenly plan.

Jesus sums up the plan in one cohesive sentence. These words weigh a ton on Peter's mind, difficult to process and assimilate into his present-day reality. The next sensible move for Peter is to offer his opinion and convince Jesus to create a more befitting, accommodating plan. *You are the Christ, Son of the living God*, after all. In Peter's mind, the Christ is more than capable of devising a plan that addresses his personal needs, as well. Unfortunately, Peter fails to understand that Jesus only does what the Father tells Him to do (John 5:19). The Father and Son relationship supersedes any earthly ties.

Peter, fixated on the impending suffering and death, neglected to ponder the words that trailed at the end, "and be raised up on the third day" (Matthew 16:21). These words landed on deaf ears unable to process any hope attached to death. Boldly, Peter professed Jesus as the Christ. Now he faced challenges in his incomplete understanding of the Christ. He saw nothing profitable in going to Jerusalem to die. Death represented finality and an unsuccessful mission. Death also meant starting all over again in identifying another to be the Christ. For Peter, the solution to this dilemma was clear to choose a route other than Jerusalem, if death awaited.

While Peter's reaction was derived from natural insights, Jesus condemning response was drawn from the spiritual realm. With Jesus Christ, sensibility was adhering to the comprehensive plan that promised His physical return to reign as King one day. Just because the plan required a painful and demoralizing death didn't alter His dedication to it. Jesus committed to move through death to advance the ultimate salvation gift and rule from His impending throne. Jesus, fully aware of His own character—life (John 14:6)—gives life (John 5:21), eternal life (John 3:15); the bread of life (John 6:35), and never allows death to intimidate Him.

With mankind, sensibility is taking measures to preserve and survive the earthly life at all costs. Naturally, our thinking is counterintuitive to God's way. His ways and thoughts are higher than ours (Isaiah 55:8-9). We discover more about God's thoughts and ways by reading and studying the Bible, but He is never fully comprehensible.

The Bible is excellent at highlighting the differences between God and man. We will never fully grasp God's thought pattern or know exactly how He arrives at His decisions. However, we will become intimately acquainted with God's heart and His love for His creation.

Paul describes Jesus as One who does "far more abundantly beyond all that we ask or think" (Eph 3:20). This is just one of Jesus' many attributes that set Him apart as God.

It is easy to condemn Peter for his impetuous response to Jesus recorded thousands of years of ago on printed pages. We may even go as far as to command Peter to stand down or deliver him a stern lecture on respect for authority. Is Peter not the mirror that reflects our images? Are we not the ones who take extra measures to avoid sacrifice or difficulties and promote self-serving agendas?

We are Peter.

I am Peter.

Awareness Exposes Our Weakness

Introspective awareness is necessary to identify yourself hidden amongst the type-written text between Jesus and Peter. Otherwise you will miss the opportunity to learn from this crucial exchange. Jesus refers to Peter as Satan, a penetrating sting (John 16:23). Peter's rebuke returns to him in the harshest, most vile way possible. Jesus exposes Peter's motivation as an alignment with Satan, an enemy. How did Peter go from being handpicked by Jesus to aligning with the enemy?

> A disciplined mind settles to listen, consider, and then speak in that order.

Somewhere along the journey with Jesus, Peter recognizes His unique heavenly traits. These traits lead Peter to proclaim Jesus as the Christ, the Son of the living God. This conclusion comes from spending time, walking, listening, and pondering Jesus. Peter collects enough evidence and opens his heart to hear from heaven. He decides that Jesus is the one to trust as savior.

Following and committing are not challenging if what I hear or see agree with my perception of reality. As soon as I detect a contrary position, I choose to bail or correct the misguided to sway over to my side.

A disciplined mind settles to listen, consider, and then speak in that order.

Peter shows us the depths of speaking without thinking. His words reprimand the Son of the living God placing himself in a lofty position that crosses all respect boundaries. Fortunately, Jesus does not calculate His movements by mistaken sways or mince words with ease. Sparing no feelings Jesus delivers a potent dose of correction. "Get behind Me, Satan! You are a stumbling block to Me . . ."(Matthew 16:23).

A stumbling block causes one to slow down, nearly trip over, or falter in moving forward. Jesus expresses clarity repeatedly in understanding what lay ahead for Him. He shows in His words and actions that nothing deters Him from making progress in pleasing the Father. A stumbling block set before Jesus will crumble into fine pieces and pose no threats.

Jesus stuns Peter with this reality check. As Peter speaks out of his self-centered flesh and blood, Jesus speaks directly to the evil influencer responsible for Peter's words, Satan. "Get behind Me, Satan" (23). For Satan, his position will always be behind Jesus. Satan will never stand ahead of or equal to Jesus.

The worst personal insult for a Jesus follower is to

be called out for entertaining the enemy. Jesus' words become a stumbling block for Peter as he trips over his own perverted thoughts and ideas. Peter proves a lack of sensitivity in discerning spiritual matters.

Discernment matures after spending time studying and applying spiritual principles. Paul prays for the Philippians, "that your love may abound still more and more in real knowledge and all discernment, so that you may approve the things that are excellent, in order to be sincere and blameless until the day of Christ" (1:9-11).

Upon hearing words that disagree with his wishes, Peter steps into an audacious role to think his way is better. Although in earlier verses, Peter's words stream from the Father who is in heaven, there is a warning here not to become complacent and rest in past accolades but remain diligent in godly pursuits and alignments. The risky alternative is to give the enemy an opportunity to persuade you into thinking that your thoughts are better than God's Words.

> *The Lord by wisdom founded the earth, by understanding He established the heavens. By His knowledge the deeps were broken up and the skies drip with dew.*
>
> *Proverbs 3:19-20*

Even if we reach the highest accomplishments during our lifetimes, we will fall short drastically in comparison to the creator. Fair and reasonable competition begins and ends between man to man.

Peter presents a prime example of how we both praise and curse God. James writes about this.

> *From the same mouth come both blessing and cursing. My brethren, these things ought not to be this way. Does a fountain send out from the same opening both fresh and bitter water? Can a fig tree, my brethren, produce olives, or a vine produce figs? Nor can salt water produce fresh.*
>
> *James 3:10-12*

James admonishes his readers not to fall prey to this behavior which overflows out of a lack of wisdom and commitment. In daily living and practice, we relegate Jesus and His plan to the background more often than not and draw attention to our personal missions.

How is this usually done? Out of ignorance. We choose not to feed upon wisdom that supplies godly guidance and direction. We seek more nourishment for the physical life while starving the spiritual. If we neglect wisdom, we look to ourselves and other ill-equipped people for the answers. Peter responds in this manner by looking to himself for a better solution.

Wisdom serves as manna from heaven with a suitable serving to last for one day. Feeding on yesterday's lessons will not build the mountainous available treasures that await dispensing. Fresh wisdom supports you to respond rightly and present in the moment without fear of what the future may bring. The future is not dismal because wisdom measures from an inexhaustible supply.

Peter's fearful response to Jesus' imminent death reflects doom and gloom for himself. When, in fact, this is liberating truth for Peter to celebrate. Jesus intends neither to exclude Peter from His future plans nor ignore the oppression that the Jews endure. Wisdom assures that God's plans are iron clad and eternally secure addressing all possible outcomes. Our role is simply to desire wisdom for our lives, daily viewing its necessity comparable to the air we breathe.

> *But if any of you lacks wisdom, let him ask of God, who gives to all generously and without reproach, and it will be given to him. But he must ask in faith, without any doubting, for the one who doubts is like the surf of the sea, driven and tossed by the wind.*
>
> *James 1:5-6*

Peter speaks without wisdom and faith. Wisdom is the precursor to developing sound faith. As Peter continues to walk with Jesus, we trace how his faith grows by clinging to wisdom. Eventually, his spiritual maturity escalates and becomes a champion of faith.

At this point, though, Jesus tells Peter that he is more

interested in himself than God (Matthew 16:23). Everyone relates to these heart-wrenching words that reign from the Garden of Eden. Our natures are identical to Eve's as believing the fruit is appealing to meet our personal needs more so than our creator. We simply need to substitute fruit for our weakness, a spouse, job, material possessions, etc. All areas we run to for momentary fulfillment. Subduing our interests to align with God's interests without a selfish slant requires effort. This is not a natural response. The sinful nature from the Garden of Eden is hungry for attention perpetually. The unending questions such as, *what about me*, *what do I get out of this*, *how do I stand to benefit*, etc. show up frequently.

It is not surprising that Peter expresses his disappointment in this manner. It is a human instinct to seek out and protect our personal agendas. As believers, we have a responsibility to squelch the questions by not giving life to egocentric agendas through our voices and behaviors. Our wants as we perceive them through selfish filters are irrelevant in comparison to God's interests. As a believer, I have assurance that God knows my wants, and His plan considers each one and includes what is best for me.

Awareness Holds Expectation

One of the traits that I appreciate, albeit painful at times, about my relationship with Jesus is how He lays my heart out before me for my own examination. Take a look. What do you see? Sometimes, I want to shrink away and hide from the ugliness and filthiness that get revealed, but Jesus is there with me in all my goriness.

And our mission together is to clean it up, not sweep it aside. I have a choice to honor my relationship by pursuing cleanliness and purity or wade in the cesspool until I choose rightly. A sinful lifestyle is comparable to taking a dip in human waste. Gross! Disgusting to think how often we accept the invitation unsuspectingly. It speaks to Satan's craftiness. He can take a cesspool and make it appear as a luxurious swimming pool filled with Caribbean blue waters at a ritzy resort surrounded by palm trees. The foul stench goes unnoticed because the false promises are intoxicating and powerful enough to disengage the sense of smell. And, sadly, we dive in and immerse ourselves completely. We spend time swimming and floating leisurely. We exit with the unsuspecting odor and invite others to come and take a dip. No matter how much we sugarcoat sin to make it more palatable, this is the reality of our choices. Sin stinks no matter how much we try to deodorize it.

During prayer which includes practicing confession, I bring my heart before God. I show Him how I dishonored His name and ask for forgiveness seeking cleanliness and purity before a holy God. Colossians 3:10-14 urges us to put on Christ, a new self that exhibits compassion, kindness, humility, gentleness, love, and so forth. There is no way that I can plant myself in sin and pursue a lifestyle that emits these traits.

> **We cannot serve God fully while clinging to our self-worth and importance.**

Putting on requires action on my part at the prompting of the Holy Spirit through the power of the Word. We cannot serve God fully while clinging to our self-worth and importance. God's interests supersede our selfish ambitions. Placing God second on our priority list is arrogance at its finest. And we, mankind, practice this flaw quite well.

The outcome is a less than productive life filled with careless and avoidable actions (sins) resulting in failed marriages, bitterness, anger, selfishness, dissension, stress, anxiety, and the list goes on. The antidote to preclude these disasters is to put God first and seek His interests through His Word.

> *Seek first His Kingdom and His righteousness, and all these things will be added to you.*
>
> *Matthew 6:33*

We cannot serve God wholly and maintain our self-worth and interests. Little by little the self-centered nature will be chiseled to reveal the masterpiece hidden within, the character of Jesus Christ. Did you think you were the masterpiece? Sorry, the artwork is not greater than the artist; the clay is not greater than the potter.

Peter's example reveals an invaluable lesson for us. Now that you have Jesus, your former way of thinking undergoes dismantling. A renewal or rebuilding of the mind takes place by feeding it biblical truths. This act appears to be easy on paper, but in practicality it is a mindset entangled with old habits and practices, refusing to adapt new ideas and principles. This process includes questioning and re-evaluating past/current decisions, suffering convictions, and resting in the promise of no condemnation.

I believe it is healthy to meander down memory lane. This trip adds appreciation for deliverance from a potentially disastrous ending. The caveat of memory lane is to partake in the stroll fully aware that Jesus is with you every step of the way. As entertaining and interesting we may find sleepwalkers, the reality is unawareness is too risky for our spiritual wellbeing. God prefers to be in a lively vibrant relationship with creation that is always aware of His presence.

Be of sober spirit, be on the alert. Your adversary, the devil prowls around like a roaring lion, seeking someone to devour.

1 Peter 5:8

Contemplation Corner:

1. Why do you think Jesus addressed Peter in such a stern tone?

2. Did the consequence fit the offence?

3. How do you behave like Peter toward Jesus?

4. Peter erred in judgment while getting to know the King. What was Peter's error?

5. How does Jesus further instruct Peter in Matthew 16:23?

6. Prior to encountering Jesus, who drives our thoughts and decisions?

7. After committing to Jesus, who seeks to drive our thoughts and decisions?

8. From Peter's example, why is it imperative to get to know Jesus?

9. Identify a time in your life in which you thought you had a better plan.

10. What was God's plan for the situation?

11. Looking back, which plan was better?

12. What are you holding on to that is intercepting Christ in your life?

13. Will you release it today?

14. Take some time to worship God as the Creator of perfect plans.

Chapter 5
Be Needy

Read Mark 10:17-22

> *As He was setting out on a journey, a man ran up to Him and knelt before Him, and asked Him, "Good Teacher, what shall I do to inherit eternal life?"*
>
> *Mark 10:17*

The man who approached Jesus hurriedly treasured his riches as the wealthy Egyptians in ancient times. The wealthy Egyptians often departed this earthly life with accumulated riches buried alongside their decaying bodies. The motivation to include their riches was to ensure continuous prestige and power in the next life.

Wealth can be hypnotizing to the point that earthly and spiritual perspectives overlap.

Those who were not concerned about the wealthy afterlife found the buried loot to be a rewarding jackpot. The looters were grave robbers who profited from the ignorance of those who had passed away. The wealthy Egyptians, absorbed in earthly matters, revealed a limited vision colored by the physical world and a lack of understanding in spiritual currency.

Recognizing a need

Wealth can be hypnotizing to the point that earthly and spiritual perspectives overlap. A healthy physical perspective identifies a neediness or emptiness that requires interaction with the spiritual realm for fulfillment. The physical points to the need for the spiritual and not vice versa. Any physical position that is unwilling to move beyond self remains stuck in a place in which there is no hope.

As enticing as it may be to carry your riches, loves and passions with you beyond the grave, the only guarantee from the physical world is death, not life. A present-day example of loyal fans choosing final rest in their alma mater coffin, highlighting allegiance to a sports team unto death, serves as lightheartedness for the mourners. But this is where the choice runs its course. This choice will not create glorious post-death moments.

The true and most sustaining passions belong to God.

The next phase for eternity offers an incomparable experience for believing fans to gather in the cheering section with premier seats. I seriously doubt those who choose Christ will long for the days of cheering for the

Aggies or Bears. The true and most sustaining passions belong to God. A spiritual perspective recognizes the significance of walking away from earthly ties at any given moment to gain everlasting profit. On the contrary, a vision that commits to the physical will cling to earthly possessions or ideologies until the final breath. Such a shallow existence delivers superficial results to the very end.

The man in this Scripture recognized a great need within himself. He sensed something was missing from his driven and successful lifestyle. While feeling a sense of security from his massive riches, the answer to an eternal life eluded him. To settle this nagging need, he employed a strategy that worked in his favor in the past. He sought advice from one who demonstrated knowledge on this subject. According to his human reasoning, he chose an expert to provide a solution for his need. The text set the tone and urgency by indicating that the man ran and knelt before Jesus. His first words addressed Jesus as "Good Teacher" (Mark 10:17).

The man was seeking to understand what was needed to inherit eternal life. Unbeknownst to the inquiring man, Jesus was the only legitimate living source with accurate and, indeed, ultimate authority to answer. The rich man underestimated the hand-picked expert by viewing Jesus as just another human with knowledge. Jesus was clearly the expert with an uppercase E. He was the final authority. The answer from Jesus was obtained from the place in which eternal life originated. To the man's credit he came to the right person to receive a foolproof, shatterproof, honest answer.

Initially, Jesus responded by focusing on the word choice, 'good.' Jesus informed the man that there was only One who was good, God. Elevating the man's thoughts pertaining to 'good' projected a greater interpretation and vision for the word. Apparently, the rich man witnessed or heard about Jesus' goodness which was a manifestation of His indwelt perfect character and righteousness. And a perfect character can only be claimed by God. Jesus emphasized this sentiment by stating, "No one is good except God alone" (18). Clearly, the man did not make the connection that he was engaging with not only a good teacher, but God incarnate.

A proper response to an encounter with God incarnate is to fall down and worship. Nevertheless, Jesus entertains the man's question while highlighting the flaws in his thinking without the rich man being the wiser. The rich man relies on human wisdom to formulate his question. His acquaintance with goodness arises from his experiences in accumulating things through self-effort. Jesus uses this opportunity to challenge the misguided thought patterns and point the way to truth. As we continue in this interaction, we will learn more about the motivations residing within his heart.

Doing vs. Being

In framing the question to Jesus, the word choice reveals a tremendous amount about his attitude toward achievement.

> *What shall I do to inherit eternal life?*
>
> *Mark 10:17*

The question lays the groundwork to begin formulating goals and a checklist. Lifestyle consultants teach us to accomplish goals by creating an action plan. Planning is an essential tool which is supported by the Bible. “The mind of man plans his way, but the Lord directs his steps” (Prov 16:9). Man has the intellectual capacity to think logically, analytically, and strategically, all components needed for effective planning. The problem becomes apparent when man relies on inherent ability to plan without inviting God to lead in creating the plan and directing his steps in the process. Man assumes both roles as planner and director foregoing a need for divine guidance. The man is seeking to set a goal and outline a path which leads to eternal life. Jesus offers a startling response to eternal life precluding 'doing' while supporting 'being.'

From a human standpoint, if you want to achieve or work toward a goal you must do something. Americans are very good at doing. We are a performance-based society. Ideally, the hard worker receives the rewards. The intent is not to bash this ideology, but to shed light on its limitations. There are some situations in which hard work does not yield dividends. This is precisely the case with eternal life.

> *For by grace you have been saved through faith; and that not of yourselves, it is the gift of God; not as a result of works, so that no one may boast.*
>
> *Ephesians 2:8-9*

The rich man attempted to apply earthly principles in obtaining wealth to acquiring eternal life. He gained success with material wealth which blinded him to the differences between the physical and spiritual realms. Those who believe that material possessions impress God and grant a favorable standing before Him never read Psalm 50:10, "For every beast of the forest is Mine, the cattle on a thousand hills." God, the Creator, owns it all so any wealth built by man on earth is minuscule to

God's riches and glories in heaven and on earth. God owns you as well as your riches. Ironically, your spiritual investments that lead to prosperity and success are the only ones that will accompany you post your physical earthly existence.

In Joshua 1:7, The Lord spoke to Joshua to instruct in the ways to success. "Only be strong and very courageous; be careful to do according to all the law which Moses My servant commanded you; do not turn from it to the right or to the left, so that you may have success wherever you go." As we seek security and answers from the world, we take hard turns and veer off course from a godly path laced with protection. Something catches our attention and causes us to look to the left or right. The glimpse to the left or right becomes a stare. Next, you are chasing after a different god with a subpar mission.

The material wealth attained while on earth will remain for others to enjoy. In examining spiritual versus physical wealth from this perspective, the principles illuminate that it is far better to expend as much if not more energy on spiritual returns. There is nothing wrong with material wealth. Wealth, as well as our gifts and talents, are intended to be used for God and by God to satisfy His purposes. After all, God owns it all. It's all about setting and adhering to priorities—Prada or Prayer.

It is a choice. Choose wisely.

Jesus answered the man's inquiry for eternal life by adding to his "not to do" list. Do not murder, commit adultery, steal, bear false witness, or defraud. Jesus also gave one positive command to honor parents. Jesus provided the man what his heart sought—the satisfaction in knowing that he was 'doing' right.

The rich man viewed his amassed wealth as proof that he must have been doing something right. Proudly standing before Jesus, the man was once again blinded by his own self-righteousness into thinking that he kept all these commandments. False gods always point to self and deliver a false sense of self-awareness.

Let's be honest—in my flesh and not considering God—I have kicked off a few people from the planet out of anger and frustration in my thoughts. Haven't you? A horrible thing to admit, but it is true.

The rich man beamed that he checked all the boxes since youth. If man can maintain morally upright behavior to be acceptable before God, then he negates the need for Jesus. He is content with his own righteousness which will never be sufficient for a meeting with a holy God. Human wisdom will mislead you to think that you are tracking well and checking boxes, but a life surrendered to God will reveal otherwise. The closer we get to God, the more we recognize our need for Him. We understand our fragility as humans. Jesus taught His disciples that even if a man looked at a woman with lust, adultery has been committed in the heart (Matthew 5:28). And as for murder, anger with a brother equated to a guilty verdict (Matthew 5:22). Jesus confirmed to the disciples that the ideas of righteousness that will satisfy their standards are insufficient and meaningless.

Jesus orchestrated the perfect setting in which the man spoke audibly deceptive words which commended his virtuous behavior. Sometimes hearing out loud what dwells in our hearts will motivate us to reexamine our beliefs. If I say silently within my heart that I am envious of another person, then I am tempted to protect and nurture my secret. If I give voice to my secret, then I am proactive in identifying my weaknesses. Releasing the secret frees me from the power and seduction that it holds over me.

Deep down, no one wants to appear weak. This is the reason we conceal our true faults and flaws from each other. We are experts at concealing and protecting our shortcomings by maintaining superficial relationships, forming impenetrable walls, and failing to connect with others. Unfortunately, these misjudgments align with Satan's strategies to hide behind a shield and disconnect from people.

I recall seeing someone who rarely said hello or smiled on a weekly basis. I knew that it was not a personal attack. Each week, I made a point to smile, attempt to engage, and compliment. My persistence chiseled away at the sheet of ice, chip by chip. Eventually, the wall fell, and I got to know her warm personality. Later, I discovered that she was afraid of forging friendships, so she closed off to protect her heart. Apparently, losing prior relationships became too much to bear, but opening her heart allowed love to flow freely. I was blessed by her letting me in. The Bible urges us to confess our sins one to another and pray for each other as these acts lead to healing (James 5:16). Satan will push us towards isolation so that he can command our full attention for his purposes.

The Heart of the Matter

Jesus directs the rich man to focus his attention on the core of the matter, his heart. Jesus resolves to showcase the false god that vied for the man's affections and divided his heart.

> *No one can serve two masters; for either he will hate the one and love the other, or he will be devoted to one and despise the other. You cannot serve God and wealth.*
>
> *Matthew 6:24*

A divided heart is incapable of pleasing God. Jesus was neither impressed with the man's possessions nor performance. "Sell all you possess and give to the poor" (Mark 10:21). Jesus attaches purpose with riches by including the poor in His statement. Riches are intended to be a source of help to others. As we help others, we extend the same compassion that characterizes Jesus.

Sell all you possess was too much to ask of someone who equated possessions with quality of life. The rich man was incapable of imagining a life that delivered as much security as his treasures. Unloading the riches overshadowed the proposition for eternal life.

While the man was accumulating wealth and experiencing success, God was continuing to move and work on his behalf by bringing other personal needs such as eternal life to his attention. God blessed the man with riches until the riches became more powerful in the man's mind. At that point, God permitted the man to choose. His riches or his God.

With a slap of terror whizzing through his heart and mind, he chose poorly. Fear gripped the man and caused him to grasp for the obvious physical choice. The riches masqueraded as a continuously satisfying royal feast when in fact the banquet table was fit for beggars and the destitute. The rich man volunteered for an existence in which there will never be enough provisions to deliver him out of his desert. He walked away grieving over his choice.

This was just the beginning of unending days filled with lack and an unquenchable thirst. A description that never left unless he chose differently later. But this was the reality of his eternity.

The man was unwilling to follow the commandment to sell and give indicated that the riches occupied a prominent attachment to his heart. The man followed the lure of misplaced affections and false promises into a deadly trap.

> *The sorrows of those who have bartered for another god will be multiplied . . .*
>
> *Psalm 16:4*

The bleak future may include additional wealth, but at what cost? What good is wealth without God's will and directions? The man will always crave more and more, probably work himself to physical exhaustion and death. The wealth, in and of itself, was not the problem. The problem arose when the owner equated wealth with security and superiority, positions reserved for God alone. The wealth became a dividing line in which God was not invited to cross or touch.

The wealth itself became powerful and began to function as a created god. The rich man operated in an ignorant sphere unaware of the price to be paid for allegiance to a false god. Eventually, the false god's voice became more attractive, though not more powerful, than the true living God to captivate the rich man's heart.

The role of any false god is to create as many barriers or distractions as possible to separate its victims from godliness and the ability to discern Truth. This aged-old trick has been around since the Garden of Eden days. Once Eve saw that the fruit was a delight to the eye for eating, she lost sight of godliness in exchange for an empty promise from Satan (Genesis 3:2-5). After experiencing God regularly in the Garden, it was difficult for Eve to pass up the chance to be like Him. Being *with* God was not enough to satisfy her flesh.

The flesh is a caloric-feasting beast, never satisfied and always making demands. The flesh seeks to replace the *missing something* with what's convenient, tangible, and sounds right for the moment. The missing *Someone* is Jesus Christ. All else is a cheap imitation who will fail every time, when disguising as the real One.

If you are deliberating over whether this is an accurate statement, I challenge you to compare your substitutes to Jesus Christ. First, you will have to admit that you are attempting to find satisfaction via solutions other than Christ. Next, it will become obvious that your created gods are not willing to endure excruciating shame and pain for your sake. At our lowest points, Jesus chooses us.

> *But God demonstrates His own love toward us, in that while we were yet sinners, Christ died for us.*
> *Romans 5:8*

Gods with a small 'g' are only in the game for the pleasure. As soon as difficulties arise, they abandon ship for a thrill with the next blinded bystander. They do not stick around to comfort, console, and help. These gods serve their best interests never yours.

Jesus masterfully displayed the rich man's heart for examination. "For if anyone thinks he is something when he is nothing, he deceives himself. But each one must examine his own work, and then he will have reason for boasting in regard to himself alone . . ." (Galatians 6:3-4). Jesus offered hope and freedom which saddened the rich man. He was unable to commit to selling his assets, giving to the poor, storing treasures in heaven, or following Jesus (Mark 10:21).

The eternal life inquiry that initiated interaction with Jesus was sacrificed and replaced by his own solution, things that fade or rust away. Choosing to walk away from a divine directive, the rich man settled for the permanent heartache that would rob him of peace, knowing that eternal life with God, according to the good Teacher, was within his grasp but cluttered by his stuff. He glimpsed the long-term vision, but due to an undisciplined heart failed to take necessary steps to rid himself of the deceiver. The rich man loved the deceiver and his offerings.

The man assessed his work as good and became content with the benefits achieved by his hands. Hard work fosters achievement, but denying God's glory repurposes accomplishments as rubbish.

Paul counted "all things to be loss in view of the surpassing value of knowing Christ Jesus" (Philippians 3:8). Paul relinquished his prestige, honor, and status as a rising defender of the Jewish faith in exchange for shipwrecks, beatings and rejections. The world viewed Paul's mental state as delusional and mad to walk away from comfort for a brutal unpredictable lifestyle. Yet, Paul never reflected on the prior comforts as a temptation to return. The encounter with Jesus Christ on the road to Damascus overshadowed the feeble possibilities left behind. Paul, emboldened by Truth, walked away from deception with unwavering courage to fulfill his calling.

In contrast to Paul, the rich man reasoned to apply learned principles in obtaining wealth to possessing eternal life. Paul released his grip on earthly possessions in pursuit of heavenly riches. He considered himself the very least of all saints, given grace to preach the unfathomable riches in Christ (Ephesians 3:8). Humbly and gratefully, Paul received his new assignment to follow and preach after encountering Jesus.

Sadly, the rich man walked away committed to unreliable wealth (here today, gone tomorrow). Paul opted for the wealth "where neither moth nor rust destroys, and where thieves do not break in or steal" (Matthew 6:20).

The question, *what must I do* reveals a mindset and heart bent towards self-effort which is a form of self-righteousness. The man was excellent at *doing*, evident by his amassed wealth. However, the rich man failed to comprehend that doing or achieving did not grant eternal life or entrance into the kingdom. In fact, it devalued the heavenly appeal. The kingdom was neither imagined nor created by man; therefore, it is precluded from susceptibility to human ingenuity.

In a parable Jesus instructed, "the kingdom of heaven is like a treasure hidden in the field, which a man found and hid again; and from joy over it he goes and sells all that he has and buys that field" (Matthew 13:44). Those who earnestly seek eternal life in the kingdom of heaven discover an invaluable treasure that arouses joy and longing.

True Goodness

Our perception of goodness, as with the rich man, gets tainted when we mix our Christian views with mainstream worldviews. For example, following the pop culture's lead, I once thought divorce for any reason was acceptable and permissible; kids were resilient to endure. After studying the Scriptures and observing some horrendous divorces, I concluded that no one wins even under the most peaceful dissolutions. The remains include fractured lives, fragile children, and unkept promises. Marriage is good for stability in families, individuals, communities, and meets God's approval. Divorce undermines the steadiness in the societal foundation for maintaining and building healthy relationships, the bedrock for civilization. The initial love that once overlooked each other's faults becomes shallow and can no longer tolerate the imperfections. The love intended for good and blessing somehow expresses itself inwardly with self-serving motives.

This love is a stark contrast to 1 Corinthians 13 which entails patience, kindness, and humility. This passage states that love never fails (8).

This same type of love was demonstrated to a fallen world by Christ. Christ went to the cross willingly for undeserved offenses. He showed profound love for us and trust in the Father for resurrection. Christ presented His life as the supreme example to emulate in understanding love. We will never get there without His help. As I listen to this deeply regarded passage read during wedding ceremonies, I understand the appeal of the poetic flow and beautiful love language. But the reality of it is unattainable without Christ. We must have Christ to teach us how to love like Him. This explains why Christ is willing to be our faithful intercessor even when we fail to recognize Him. Christ does all from His perfect nature which is grounded in love.

Wealth can be used for many good opportunities to express God's love for His creation. But once wealth becomes self-serving, the good is wasted on personal missions. The worldview of wealth becomes entangled with the godly view causing the blessing to become stagnant instead of an outward flow to others. The beaver builds a dam for self-serving purposes, his own housing and safety. As a result of the dam, the water flow takes on a different path than its original intent. Just as a dam will slow the water flow and divert the direction, so will receiving a blessing and determining that you are the ultimate benefactor. A self-server who lacks God's vision and heart intercepts divine flow.

The rich man was proficient and excelled in worldly maneuvers but lacked in the spiritual matters. The rich man failed to protect his most valuable asset, his heart. This lack of boundary provided an opportunity for the false god to enter and take up residency. The false god wreaked sufficient havoc to veil the rich man's need for a Savior. He was content to contend with the false god's occupancy which impacted the mind and heart to embrace Truth.

Unfortunately, the rich man was perverted in his thinking by interchanging spiritual and worldly principles. The world endorses doing good to earn or receive. The spiritual realm where eternal life resides declares that you will never claim ownership by earnings or efforts. The spiritual realm represents holiness and righteousness established by God. Working or self-effort will never be good enough or the prerequisite to be acceptable in God's sight. The rich man was unable to abandon the worldly ways that crept into his life. He walked away saddened by his decision to retain present wealth over future riches. The grave consequence meant walking away from his Lord to seek comfort from material things that are incapable of providing the relief he needs. Beliefs in Jesus and His agenda protect us from becoming acquainted with this type of sadness as we live to express outwardly the fruit of the Spirit (Galatians 5:22-23).

Jesus says, "Why are you asking Me about what is

good? There is only One who is good . . ." (Matthew 16:17). The fallacy in assuming that man's nature contains goodness apart from his Maker epitomizes absurdity. The rich man addresses Jesus as just another man. He probably considers his riches sufficient proof that he is worthy to be in the good Teacher's presence. His wealth is noteworthy to another man but fails to reach the heights of God's standards for goodness. It is impossible to attain approval or acceptance by God through personal work or material possessions.

Jesus corrected this thinking and made the rich man aware that he appropriated goodness to mankind when the attribute can only be claimed by God. Jesus gives the man a clue that his alignment leans spiritually by pointing to God. The clue slides past the man like a baseball player stealing second base. Clueless to the spiritual realm, the rich man makes choices that gratify in the moment. His focus fixates on material possessions and he walks away in the same condition without his need being met.

Thankfully, we live daily with the Holy Spirit who scours the heart to protect us from false gods. Now that Jesus is a part of our lives, we take measures to fill our hearts with Him so that the enemy will not entice us to follow a different god. We adhere to the spiritual principles that keep us pleasing and acceptable. The key component to building spiritual riches is consistency in making God a priority. Not only to say the words but follow up with actions. As we set aside time to study God's Word daily, we build spiritual resilience and become stronger in defending off satanic tactics.

An unhealthy approach to material wealth leads to hoarding. A healthy attitude understands that God's provisions are inexhaustible. Anything that attempts to compete with spiritual wealth is worthless regardless of the promising prestige. True value comes from knowing and loving God. The goal is for nothing to hinder this relationship. By doing this, we rest in the assurance that our neediness is being met with an abundance of godly provisions.

> *And my God will supply all your needs according to His glorious riches in Christ Jesus.*
>
> *Philippians 4:19*

Contemplation Corner

1. What are you 'doing' that qualifies you as good?

2. How have you denounced self-righteousness?

3. What or Who makes you righteous (standing rightly, acceptable before God) to stand in God's presence?

4. Why is it necessary to be righteous?

5. What is vying for your attention and affection leaving a void in which God should be occupying?

6. What role does wealth play in your life?

7. Do you agree that the flesh is weak and subject to temptations? Identify your weaknesses.

8. What steps are you actively taking to strengthen the Spirit's presence and weaken the flesh?

9. Are you experiencing a lack of peace? What is the root cause for this experience?

10. What is the best way to pursue a peaceful life?

11. What motivates you to work diligently at your workplace? At your church?

12. How do you think the world has impacted your kingdom views and thinking?

13. How will you set boundaries to filter the worldviews from your Christian views that are grounded in Biblical truths?

Chapter 6
Be Open

Read John 4:3-30

> *The woman said to Him, "Sir, give me this water, so I will not be thirsty nor come all the way here to draw." He said to her, "Go, call your husband and come here." The woman answered and said, "I have no husband." Jesus said to her, "You have correctly said, 'I have no husband'; for you have had five husbands and the one whom you now have is not your husband; this you have said truly." The woman said to Him, "Sir, I perceive that You are a prophet. Our fathers worshiped in this mountain, and you people say that in Jerusalem is the place where men ought to worship." Jesus said to her, "Woman, believe Me, an hour is coming when neither in this mountain nor in Jerusalem will you worship the Father.*
>
> *John 4:15-21*

Have you ever compared your life to a scene in the movie Groundhog Day? Did you think the writer had you in mind when envisioning this movie? This highly entertaining and comical movie dealt with Bill Murray's need to change by scripting him to live the same day repeatedly. His yesterday and today began and concluded the exact same way for numerous days spanning over years. His life was unfolding at a standstill in time on a perpetual hamster wheel. The repetition forced the character to reevaluate his ways. Eventually, a transformation occurred from a narcissistic angry demeanor to a lesser self-centered nature. His ability to escape the time-warped loop was contingent upon him demonstrating his desire to improve as a human being.

This movie relates well to the human experience. It is a common occurrence to find yourself in a similar situation staring down the same results continually. Puzzled and mystified at your arrival at this familiar predicament once again. Relationships are prime examples of a repetitive loop in attracting the same character flaws that you desire to desperately avoid. Yet, somehow these flaws follow you around and become guests in your personal space. Only for you to discover later that you met that person earlier. The only differences are the name and face, but identical character traits. It is as frustrating as shooing away a persistent nagging fly. You feel sideswiped and perplexed by your choices.

> Until we learn that personal fulfillment is not the responsibility of another human, we continue this exhausting search for the next bewildered prospect who holds worthless promises that guarantee security.

Deep down you notice a longing or yearning that always seems to persist. This feeling is agitating and gnaws away at your soul robbing it of peace and security. You open your heart and arms to anyone who hints at resolving this personal disturbance, completely unaware that this person has similar gnaws that need addressing. Both will become equally frustrated and impatient with each other's inability to meet their needs.

Until we learn that personal fulfillment is not the responsibility of another human, we continue this exhausting search for the next bewildered prospect who holds worthless promises that guarantee security.

The Samaritan woman at the well teaches us this lesson poignantly. As she opens her heart to a complete stranger at the well, she allows us as readers a chance to hold her hand and say, me too. Unless of course, you are in denial. You may not relate to multiple spouses or partners. The intent to meet and fill your need may surface in performance-based personalities, seeking approval from others, addictions, over-zealous competitive natures, etc. This list is not exhaustive, but everyone's name is on a list. The Samaritan woman is clearly looping with multiple partners. But as with Bill Murray, her loop separates after she learns and accepts a different way to fulfillment. Jesus visits a less desirable city to meet a less desirable woman for the sake of this fulfillment.

An Unthinkable Place

Of all the places available to Jesus, He chose little ole Samaria. A town that was not appropriate for a proper Jew to visit due to its misfit inhabitants. It was not uncommon for Jews to travel extra distances to avoid this city. Samaria was populated with a community of mixed races and faiths. The problem arose when the people intermingled and married. The Jews who lived in this land married foreigners of different faiths and produced offspring. Jews were warned not to marry foreigners as the potential to serve a different god was too great. And this was happening in Samaria. People were serving the God of Israel as well as stirring other religious beliefs in the pot. These practices infuriated the strict Jews who remained committed to protecting their heritage and obeying the Law. The Jews identified this lifestyle as despicable and avoided it as much as possible.

Jesus with a proper Jewish lineage was not deterred by the mixed heritages and religious beliefs. His commitment to delivering truth prohibited Him from isolating any community from receiving Him. Jesus understood man's wandering and impulsive natures that were easily enticed to follow a perishing path. His plan was to engage, rescue, and save that person from destruction. Jesus interacted with the elite and educated religious Jewish groups as well. Unfortunately, many from this group rejected Jesus and His teachings. And this group viewed the Samaritans as unclean, best left ignored and untouched. Some Jews lived in disobedience to their faith which ascribed that the God of Israel was the true living God for all nations.

Throughout Jesus' ministry, He never cowered away from the untouchables. In His mind, all sinners were untouchables prompting the need for His earthly visitation. A spoken word or eye contact was the precise touch people yearned for then and today. Jesus wanted to see, feel, and listen to hearts to identify as a sympathetic Savior. "For we do not have a high priest who cannot sympathize with our weaknesses, but One who has been tempted in all things as we are, yet without sin" (Hebrews 4:15). Jesus found people who wanted to be touched in Samaria.

Let's face it, there is a little bit of Samaria in each of us. The mixed-up Samaritans made the Jews with a pure lineage uncomfortable. In addition, the Samaritans' knowledge of God was limited and shaped by the first five books of what we know as the Bible today. However, their limitations did not prevent them from hoping for a Messiah to come. The Samaritans believed in a Messiah who would come to them and explain God. Jesus came and fulfilled their desires to know Him, to know Truth. How are we like the Samaritans? We are a mixed-up people who continue to make the self-righteous uncomfortable. The Samaritans teach us that Jesus loves us in spite of ourselves.

An Unthinkable Woman

The Samaritan woman carried out her routine just as any other ordinary day. She made her way to the well alone without the company of other women. This day was no exception from any other day. She was no stranger to loneliness or tolerating the heat during the sixth hour of the day. She was accustomed to satisfying her own thirsty needs each day by trekking to Jacob's well for water. Today was the same as yesterday and previous days passed.

Except, this time when she reached the well, a Jewish man was resting there. What was more extraordinary from any other day, the Jewish man asked her a question. It was common law for a Jewish man to regard a Samaritan woman as one who was always menstruating. There was no way that a self-respecting Jew would put himself in a position to engage this woman. The unfavorable odds against her were too compelling—woman, Samaritan, ostracized by her own people, unclean by law, blatantly sinful. She was the woman known by more labels than her birth name.

Jesus sent all the disciples away to purchase supplies. Thinking ahead, He welcomed no objections to this divine appointment. Jesus understood that the woman who bore all these labels appeared unscathed by life circumstances. But underneath the protective layers lived a scarred, fragile, tender-hearted little girl who was searching. She was too precious to submit to the microscopic scorn that one of the disciples might imply. So, He sent them away and waited for the Samaritan woman to arrive at the well to satisfy her physical thirst. The wait was pregnant with anticipation of the pending reconstruction soon to take place. God has the power to reconstruct the effects of our brokenness, burdens, shame, and hurt for His purposes and our good.

God has the power to reconstruct the effects of our brokenness, burdens, shame, and hurt for His purposes and our good.

One of the most comforting aspects of Jesus' encounter with the Samaritan woman involves His intentional waiting for her to arrive. This posture frees us from the enemy's tactics in deceiving us to believe that God has little time for us. This preordained meeting teaches us differently. Jesus waits for the woman patiently. He engages with her tenderly without consideration of her heritage, past sins, or current ones. Jesus demonstrates loving concern for the Samaritan woman in her present state and the choice being made available to her within this divine moment. He shuts down all other voices to create an atmosphere that invites the only opinion that matters, God's.

> *The Lord is not slow about His promise, as some count slowness, but is patient toward you, not wishing for any to perish but for all to come to repentance.*
>
> *2 Peter 3:9*

Jesus continues to comfort us with this same trait today. His consistency builds and shapes our faith. He is the same yesterday and today.

I am like the bratty child who wants her way. Sometimes, my stubbornness and determination to occupy the driver's seat blind me to Jesus waiting for me. I cannot sense His presence or hear His voice. I only hear my overwhelmingly unruly thoughts replaying the same reel over and over.

He waits for me to move past the tantrum so that He may have His say. And each time His offer involves peace, love, joy, and all those fruits that represent His Spirit. Jesus offers security and assurance that can only be found in Him. Just as Jesus waits on us, there is a promise for me if I change my behavior and wait on Him.

> *Yet those who wait for the Lord will gain new strength.*
>
> *Isaiah 40:31b*

I love how this encounter involves Jesus waiting for the woman to arrive. It makes me think of times known and unknown that Jesus waited on me. It speaks to His patience and timing. It confirms that Jesus does not operate on man's timetable. He is not deterred by our wrong choices or what others think about us. He waits for the ideal moment which may occur at the most mundane time of the day. His timing does not require fanfare or pomp and circumstance although He is worthy of that preparation. His mission is to present an open heart with a life changing message that will meet a specific need.

An Unthinkable Request

The Samaritan woman approached the well, taking notice of her surroundings. She was not hesitant in drawing water with a man nearby. She was minding her business until the man asserted Himself into her day by making a request. The request was, "Give Me a drink"

(John 4:7).

The woman fired back demonstrating her knowledge of the common law. She was aware and accepting of her labels and place in society. She created no waves with her social status. Why bother fighting others when the fight for your life was at stake? She knew the thoughts that Jewish men directed towards her. There was no pretentiousness in her response. "How is it that You, being a Jew, ask me for a drink since I am a Samaritan woman?" (9). The Samaritan woman's direct and straight-forward response revealed her openness to hear what this Jewish Man had to say.

An Unthinkable Offer

Jesus opens the dialogue by asking the Samaritan woman for a drink. He ignores all man-made stigmas associated with this uncommon exchange. At the same time, Jesus reminds the woman of the disgraces that haunt her daily not for the sake of hurling guilt, but to set in motion the deliverance plan. The offer that is coming her way will eradicate the weight of her public humiliations. After interacting with Jesus, her cumbersome overbearing afflictions will lose their heaviness. She will soon discover that she will no longer need to carry her burdens alone. In fact, she will not need to carry them at all as she chooses to walk in freedom with a fresh boldness.

Jesus intends to steer her attention away from what others may think or say about her. He wants to silence their erroneous voices to lead her to what is worthwhile. In fact, race and/or religion relations are noises attempting to steal attention away from the true matter at hand. Associating or disassociating with one race or the other lends no credence to spiritual awareness. This choice only affirms the depravity of the human heart without God. How much precious time gets wasted promoting self-serving agendas all in the spirit of pleasing God? We deceive ourselves into thinking that we are carrying out God's plans on His behalf as ambassadors.

> *For the time will come when they will not endure sound doctrine, but wanting to have their ears tickled, they will accumulate for themselves teachers in accordance to their own desires, and turn away their ears from the truths and will turn aside to myths.*
>
> *2 Timothy 4:3-4*

It was as though Jesus was saying, "Do not worry that I am a Jew and you are a Samaritan. Do not consume yourself with past self-defeating choices and empty liberating promises. Those facts are insignificant in defining this present moment." Most pressing in this sacred moment is Jesus asking for a drink as the first step in chipping away at a cracked façade. Ironically, Jesus uses His request for a drink to satisfy a physical need as a prelude to offering living water to quench her spiritual thirst. His brilliant omniscience is on display prominently. And we are in awe of its effects.

Putting distance between His request for water and the woman's response, Jesus moves forward to challenge her thinking. He suggests the more appropriate questions are, "Who are you? What is the gift of God? What is living water?" And possibly one question deriving from her personal experience is, "How does any of this provide a remedy for me fetching water during the heat of the day?"

Nevertheless, the Samaritan woman presses onward with other questions. "Where is your cup? What will you draw the water with? Why are you unprepared?" These questions reveal that her current thoughts reflect her lifestyle. One that is built upon bringing satisfaction to her physical and natural needs.

Since her focus is on the physical surroundings, Jesus draws a distinction between the power of His water and Jacob's water. "If you drink Jacob's water, you will thirst again. Jacob's water has the power to satisfy momentarily. The water that I am offering provides unending satisfaction without any interferences ever."

Thinking naturally, she considers not having to walk to the well, deal with public scrutiny, or endure varying temperatures. The urge to accept this offer becomes stronger and stronger. The woman gladly declares her longing for Jesus to resolve her physical needs. After all, she is a woman who seeks others to fulfill her personal needs. She is no stranger to men making these kinds of offers to her. And she is no stranger to accepting offers from men. But unlike her past encounters, she has not met a stranger like Jesus before.

Jesus sensing that the Samaritan woman has not fully grasped the meaning in the moment, He pivots to the next attention-grabbing statement. "Go, call your husband and come here"(John 4:16).

What do you do when the past refuses to leave? No matter where you go, it tags along like an unrelenting toothache. You find yourself wanting to scream, "just leave me alone". If a hurtful past were a tangible object, flinging it off a harrowing cliff, stomping upon its final death sounds gratifying. Unfortunately, this is not the way to puncture the inflated power from a haunting past.

The Samaritan woman demonstrates the most mature way to deal with a less than ideal history. First, she acknowledges the past even though it continues to show up in her present. Secondly, she speaks truthfully concerning her past and chooses not to hide under the covers of shame. Thirdly, she expresses the past in a manner that assumes complete personal responsibility for her actions. With a sincere sin-stained heart, the Samaritan woman speaks, “I have no husband” (17).

Proof that Jesus is open to receive our confessions, He affirms her truth. Jesus does not reprimand or shovel more reasons for her to thirst. He continues to nudge her tenderly towards a safe passage to follow Him. With the following words Jesus lets her know that it is indeed safe to be a Samaritan speaking to a Jew, “You have correctly said, ‘I have no husband;’ for you have had five husbands, and one whom you now have is not your husband; this you have said truly” (17-18). Jesus knows her past, present, and the bountiful future that awaits. He stands still without flinching in her presence while carrying out the engagement intentionally.

Jesus sends a message that no sin is too great for Him to conquer and break the bond. He commits to finishing His mission and rescuing her soul from the undermining evil one. This one engagement with Jesus contains enough power to shut down the roll call for future husbands and men. After this encounter, their services will not be needed to fulfill their self-serving agendas at her expense. She will be whole and no longer available for a broken sinner to stand in as a poor substitute for her God.

How shocking for the Samaritan woman to be speaking to a complete stranger who knows her personal past. I am so grateful that she did not try and paint an alternative to her truth or make excuses. She did not attempt to blame others, the men, her childhood, her parents, or geography. These unproductive tactics drive the pain into a deeper well of despair. She confesses from her sheer reality platform. It is what it is. It is as raw as it sounds. This confession opens and prepares the heart to receive a soothing salve for her aching soul.

The Samaritan woman's needs present themselves physically in a man/husband form repeatedly. The yearning which resides deep within reaches for that form each time with false hopes that this time will be different. The clues lead us to believe that her needs are for a husband who is willing to protect, lead, guide, be faithful, truthful, and forever present. Fortunately for her, Jesus meets all these qualifications plus others. Jesus intends to assure her that He is more than qualified to be her husband and more. She will no longer seek a man to satisfy that of which only God is capable.

Stunned at the details that Jesus revealed to her, the Samaritan woman assumes that Jesus must be a prophet. She expresses hope in the Messiah who will come one day and make known all truths. Somehow through all the disappointments and setbacks, she clings to hope in a coming Messiah. Her background fits perfectly in preparing Samaria to receive a Savior. Her lifestyle depicts the hearts of many who search for answers while failing to achieve ultimate satisfaction.

The drive to seek relief after each disappointment is as addictive as a drug habit. Just as a drug addict does not volunteer for a lifetime of misery, neither does a sinner. At least, the next high provides a temporary escape for the addict. The sinner always remains encased in darkness.

> *[Jesus says,] "I am the Light of the world; he who follows Me will not walk in darkness, but will have the Light of life."*
>
> *John 8:12*

Jesus enlightens her that He is the long-awaited Messiah. The Messiah is present to release her from her personal bondage and serve as "Savior of the world" (John 4:42).

Immediately, joy and excitement overtake the Samaritan woman as she realizes her proximity to salvation and deliverance. She witnesses and interacts with the Messiah who has not forgotten about His visitation. Never in her wildest dreams, did she ever anticipate her participation in the Messiah's arrival to Samaria. Surely others are more worthy and outwardly polished for this royal visit.

An Unthinkable Ending

The Samaritan woman releases her attachment to the natural world, by dropping the waterpot. With extreme clarity, she proceeds into the city to share the good news. "Come and see. Is this the Christ we have been waiting for?" (29). The waterpot, temperature, and reputation all appear to be irrelevant with one simple declaration, "I who speak to you am He" (26). A casual conversation turns into the most important words in a lifetime.

Actually, a lifetime is too limiting. Jesus' words carry eternal weight since "He is the image of the invisible God, the firstborn of all creation. For by Him all things were created, both in the heavens and on earth, visible and invisible, whether thrones or dominions or rulers or authorities—all things have been created through Him and for Him" (Colossians 1:15-16).

Imagining her thought process, "the long-hoped-for Messiah knows me personally and all that entails." She gets a Messiah who engages her unhurriedly with thought provoking words. She appears before her Messiah without a hint of condemnation. This moment marks her wholeness, her fulfillment. She has her Messiah who has come and explained everything to her.

Jesus' encounter with the Samaritan woman paints Him as a patient, loving, tender, careful Christ. He wants to expose our needs and show how He is the only One who qualifies to meet them.

The Samaritan woman is my dear friend. I admire her courage to continue teaching lessons on living a condemnation-free life. She teaches boldly how to walk away from the past, into the present and onward into the future. This shines as the example for countless followers, myself included.

If you are a person without a colored past, congratulations. For those of us with a past filled with repeatedly poor choices, the Samaritan woman is our she-ro. In my 20's, I had a difficult time making healthy choices for myself. Always seeming to be attracted to the wrong guy for the wrong reason. And how did he always seem to find me. I remember finding myself in precarious situations and uttering, 'not again'. My situation was not limited to male companionship. It was female friendships, finances, education, etc. No matter how hard I sought to resolve various scenarios, my remedies were not sufficient to deliver me from unnecessary heartaches. Until one day, it all changed. I met the Messiah. Unlike the Samaritan woman, I was not expecting Him or holding out hope for His arrival. Apparently, He was expecting me. But just like the

Samaritan woman, He waited patiently for me. He handled me very tenderly, leading me to Truth as a student, in a manner that spoke to me directly. He sent me to His Word with qualified, patient women surrounding me. As one with a studious inquisitive nature, He sat me before Him page after page—reading, underlining, scribbling, thinking, and answering questions for a year. I rarely missed a class, if any. I was on the greatest pursuit of my life. And similar to the Samaritan woman, I was naïve to think that it was just another ordinary experience.

At the conclusion of my study, I, too, dropped my water bucket. I cannot say that my past was instantly behind me. But the journey began to release the weight. I began to understand that my needs were spiritual in nature and not physical. Yet, I was seeking the physical for my answers. The physical provided answers that added to my woes never lightening them. I stopped consulting the physical world for my spiritual needs.

Jesus says that He is the Light. I will not find Him in darkness. I was deceived to believe that the darkness wanted to help me, when the darkness only exists to destroy. God revealed Himself to me inclusive of a sordid past with no condemnation and forgetfulness. He remembers my sins no more. And neither do I.

Jesus is willing. He is willing to come and visit each

one personally. He is not deterred by our experiences and disappointments. If we permit the world to become too active in our affairs, it will interfere with our ability to see God and love Him. As much as the enemy attempts to blind us to God, his powers are limited. God demonstrates His love for creation from Genesis to Revelation. His love covers from sunrise to sunset. The timeline initiates before your physical existence and will endure into everlasting. These thoughts are incomprehensible with physical sight and closed-mindedness. Spiritual awareness elevates your thinking to embrace faith. With faith comes an openness to accept truth and live accordingly. Jesus boldly proclaims it.

> *and you will know the truth, and the truth will make you free.*
>
> *John 8:32*

Contemplation Corner:

1. What sin are you too ashamed to admit today?

2. Do you recognize shame as a tactic from the enemy?

3. What steps will you take to step outside of shame towards freedom today?

4. Do you know Jesus as a patient and tender Savior?

5. What words do you use to describe Jesus?

6. Are you encouraged by the Samaritan woman's openness and truthfulness?

7. What did you learn from her accepting the past?

8. Have you experienced the living water?

9. How did your thirst reveal itself?

10. Recall when you realized that the living water quenched your thirst.

11. The Samaritan woman went to tell others about her encounter. Why do you think she was compelled to share with others?

12. How do you share your encounter?

13. Are you open to embracing an ongoing encounter with Jesus?

Chapter 7

Be Sensitive to the Presence of God

Read Luke 10:38-42

> *Martha, Martha, you are worried and bothered about so many things; but only one thing is necessary, for Mary has chosen the good part, which shall not be taken away from her.*
>
> *Luke 10:41-42*

The harried life. We all fall prey to its talons. Imperfectly juggling activities and tasks. Missing one toss only to stoop, pick up, and start the juggle all over. We want off the carnival ride but don't take the moment to alert the operator of our desire to disembark. We become caught up in a fast-paced lifestyle without realizing that an alternative is available. Outside demands scream the loudest and receive immediate attention.

I recall a personal family experience with an outcome that fits perfectly in this frazzled lifestyle. My brother announced his wedding plans. How excited we were to celebrate a major milestone with him. However, as parents with three young children, celebrations took on a different meaning especially with air travel.

This particular trip was similar to all others in our past travels. You would think we learned and improved. We pledged an exhausted vow after each trip. The pledge lasted as long as our sighs. Working, parenting, managing the home left no time to practice effective time management. We rushed to get things done at the last minute. Frantic with anxieties, we headed off to the airport, probably lingered a bit too long this time, but my husband with frightening driving skills did whatever required to get us to the airport on time.

Upon airport arrival, there were other concerns—curbside check-in, car seats, diaper bags, three children ages five and under, and just as important, the budget-friendly remote parking. After being dropped off at the airport with two kids and the diaper bag, husband scurried off to execute the second phase of celebrate-brother's-wedding plan. We boarded the plane and waited for the remaining two-fifths to join us. The final announcement to close the doors sounded troubling to me.

Three of us made the flight to Atlanta while two remained stunned in defeat. It had worked so well in the past. Did I mention that I had the diaper bag for the baby who missed the flight? No food. No diapers. No cell phones. The only saving grace was hubby traveled with the calmest child of the three.

By the time we all came together again, the celebratory notions waned to longings for a nap. Family members wasted no time laughing at our expense, referring to us as the Texas Rangers affectionately. We earned a reputation of living a mind-boggling lifestyle which was addicted to adrenaline-fueled decisions.

Throughout the trip, we pressed through with an endgame to show up as one well-put-together, loving family. The plan fell apart due to lack of focus, discipline, planning, etc. Our attention was preoccupied by other competing matters that diverted us away from impending deadlines. Living on a get-it-done mentality led to frustrations that overshadowed a treasurable moment. As much as we identified with Martha and her busy nature, we secretly yearned for Mary.

The Good Part

Mary masters associating with the good part. The good part of a criminal court case is prevailing justice. The good part of Cinderella is the glass slipper fitting the foot of the rightful owner. The good part of Jesus is in His totality. There is no subdividing to get to the good stuff. He is all good. Mary chooses to be near Jesus in all His goodness. And her choice rewards her with affirming words from her Savior implying that she made the best decision ever. The Psalmist agrees with Mary and proclaims, "But as for me, the nearness of God is my good" (Psalm 73:28).

Jesus ministered for three short years. His days were numbered. Firmly grounded in His mission, He did not have the option to extend His stay beyond the established time. One of those precious moments were spent in Mary and Martha's home. Mary and Martha were privileged to receive a personal visit. Interestingly, each responded to the visit in a different manner. Mary rested at Jesus feet and listened. Martha busied herself to extend exceptional hospitality to her guest. Both approaches included time-sensitivity, but each interpreted the moment in strikingly opposite ways. The focus on getting things done led to frustrations rather than fulfillment. Sitting and listening yielded a compliment from Jesus and impressions that lasted a lifetime. Many years after this time with Jesus, any heartaches or disappointments will be comforted with this unforgettable moment. His healing words will continue to flow with almighty strength and power long after this moment ceased. Mary assumed a posture with a proximity to holiness that many dreamed but few experienced.

Mary and Martha offer prime examples of how we tend to respond to God. Either we love on Him wholeheartedly or become easily distracted doing good for His namesake. And in our distraction, we want others to become distracted as well. Misery loves company. At first glance, we ascertain Mary's love for Jesus. A second look confirms that Martha loves Jesus too. She shows her love by diving headfirst into an elaborate hostess role which requires many steps to carry out. Either Martha is driven to impress her guest with Martha Stewart type talent or she is caught up in the moment with numerous tasks. The focus on lesser important matters has the potential to add up to a costly distraction. With today's labeling and research, we can safely identify Martha's love language as acts of service.

Distracted Living

Martha creates a plan that is beyond her capabilities. She needs assistance from Mary who has different priorities. Initially, Martha has a fantastic plan to serve her Lord with the highest honors in her home. Martha's choices are relatable to anyone who invites others into their home.

An important guest in my home warrants a checklist and visit to the Home Goods store. Once I invited a group over to my home as an end-of-the-year gathering. I put in considerable time in constructing an eye-catching table setting with appealing food selections. After much energy and thinking about entertaining these guests, they arrived and preferred paper products. I forgot all about my plans and enjoyed the thought-provoking conversations which taught me to cherish people and not the process or products.

For Martha, a downward spiral begins once she recognizes that her plans are too grand for even her. She searches without thinking for available hands to assist in fulfilling her wishes. Without processing her thoughts, she disrupts Jesus and Mary to assert what she deems as her most pressing need. Martha needs for Mary to leave Jesus for a pot that awaits in the kitchen. However, Martha's most pressing need is to be at Jesus' feet as well.

Martha's self-absorption with her plans leads her to accuse Jesus of not caring about her. "Lord, do You not care that my sister has left me to do all the serving alone?" (Luke 10:40). Martha understands that Jesus holds an authoritative position as she refers to Him as Lord. But Martha's words thunder for Jesus to exercise subordination to her whims and demands. "Lord, don't you care . . .?" No one will ever care more than Jesus about all details of life including hosting. Clearly, Martha drowns in details and loses sight of the big picture. The big picture screams Jesus is with her in this very moment.

Selfishness creeps into Martha's thinking which assumes that she knows what is best for Jesus while addressing her own needs. Turns out that Jesus is fine with cheese and crackers, a lesser fanfare with more simplicity. Jesus wants Martha to embrace the opportunity more than her preparations.

After Martha chastises Jesus for not caring, she proceeds to instruct Him on how to handle this botched situation. "Then tell her to help me." (Luke 10:40). Insight into Martha's words reveals that she is completely committed to her hosting plans, blinded to any other activities or purposes. The remaining tasks on the to-do list project just enough power to cause her to become unaware of the present moment. Physically her body is in the room with Jesus, but her mind focuses on the future, mealtime. Martha is driven by her perceived end results—the perfect meal for her guests. Shallow plans, even with good intentions, can only propagate superficiality. Jesus takes advantage of this opportunity to teach Martha an invaluable lesson.

Shallow plans, even with good intentions, can only propagate superficiality.

Martha tells Jesus what to do and the best way to

resolve her issue. Clearly, she forgets to whom she is speaking. An awkward moment in which the clay begins to speak to the potter. A moment that is comparable to the belligerent child who knows more than the parent. The only gesture that Martha gets right in this situation is going to Jesus with her frustrations.

> *Therefore humble yourselves under the mighty hand of God, that He may exalt you at the proper time, casting all your anxiety on Him, because He cares for you.*
>
> *1 Peter 5:6-7*

No doubts exist that Jesus cares for Martha. Jesus demonstrates His love for Martha in a few ways. He accepts her invitation to come into her home. Jesus listens to Martha's concerns. And Jesus addresses those concerns with specific language to redirect her focus. Jesus' choices are unlimited. And He chooses Martha and her home. Martha believes she is loving Jesus at her finest, but her actions speak otherwise. Truth resides in the outpouring from the heart. What flows from Martha's heart equates to a restlessness as she expresses her love language.

Jesus observes that so many things are bothering Martha. A joyous occasion turns into a hassle for the host. Jesus' presence then and now serves to protect us from worldly influences. The power of His presence shields us from such nuisances by empowering us to love Jesus more than the world. But the shield only works if we choose to acknowledge and wear it.

> *In addition to all, taking up the shield of faith with which you will be able to extinguish all the flaming arrows of the evil one.*
>
> *Ephesians 6:16*

Overcommitting without guidance from a godly perspective promotes self-gratification. Checking off multiple boxes on a spiritual checklist aligns with a works-based mentality versus grace. Negative outward responses such as outbursts and gut-wrenching inward feelings are clear indicators as to which is being engaged. The danger in abandoning godly principles for more worldly influences invites emotional instability and a lack of discipline with words and actions.

How did Martha find herself in this predicament? One misbehaved thought challenged her plan, and she began to panic. It only took one thought linked to doubt to initiate a mental downward spiral. Martha began to feel the pressure that her plan was not working. That thought led her grasping for solutions to breathe life back into her unwarranted plans. With a judgment clouded by misguided thoughts, she lashed out at whatever or whomever were available at the moment, Jesus and

Mary.

An Intervention

Jesus intervened to rescue Martha from herself, her thoughts, and the enemy attempting to intercept a glorious moment. The enemy was certain he found an opportunity through Martha to create dissension, disrupt relationships, and circumvent Mary, serving as an example of how to love Jesus unashamedly, perfectly. Jesus overcame the enemy by restoring order and calmness to Martha and correcting her thinking. Jesus handled Martha with His preferred method of caring for His own. He corrected her tenderly with compassion and never condemnation.

Jesus, with keen sensitivities, simultaneously appreciated Mary and observed Martha. His conclusions summed up Martha as having so many things bothering her (Luke 10:41), not just the meal preparations. The purpose for Jesus accepting Martha's invitation was not only to enjoy her meal, but to leave her with life-altering insights. Jesus was intentional in mending Martha's fractured heart, pulled in many directions by overly appraised tasks. Tasks that aroused more tension than necessary. A crafty perpetrator slithered his way to

> Mary sat while Martha scurried.

Martha with intentions to prevent her from embracing a magnificent experience, spending time with her Lord.

The enemy chose not to pursue Mary or found no entrance to invade. No foothold (Ephesians 4:27). Mary understood how to assess the moment and prioritize. She observed the same scenarios as Martha swirling around her but reacted startlingly different. Mary chose to be "seated at the Lord's feet, listening to His word" (Luke 10:39), and refused to be pulled away. Mary sat while Martha scurried. Mary exhibited calmness during Martha's frenzy. Mary witnessed the chaotic preparations without participating while Martha succumbed to pressures to perform. Martha cried out a plea for help. Mary was silent, relishing in contentment without a conceivable need. Jesus confirmed the power contained in the ability to choose. "Mary has chosen the good part, which shall not be taken away from her" (42). The enemy was unable to manipulate Mary because she chose the good part and received protection from his tactics.

Everyday we face choices that facilitate us entertaining the enemy or Jesus Christ. The enemy has a knack for making a situation appear bigger and more imposing than reality. Suddenly, the fruit in the garden appears more delicious than days before. God's presence in the Garden with daily fellowship diminishes in value and becomes less significant. He distorts the truth masterfully.

Jesus proves in his interactions with Mary and Martha that by choosing Him the benefits are indisputable. Jesus chooses to love us from His unchangeable nature.

> *Jesus Christ is the same yesterday and today and forever.*
>
> *Hebrews 13:8*

He has no plans to deceive or misrepresent truth to us. He is good and only wants good for His followers. Jesus provides a blanket assurance to Mary and Martha by stating that Mary's choice has everlasting impact. Not only does Jesus stand by His word, He follows up with action. He speaks for today and into eternity.

Paul agrees in one of his letters.

> *For I am convinced that neither death, nor life, nor angels, nor principalities, nor things present, nor things to come, nor powers, nor height, nor depth, nor any other created thing, will be able to separate us from the love of God, which is in Christ Jesus our Lord.*
>
> *Romans 8:38-39*

The enemy proposes a temptation in which he can use to create a barrier between a believer and Jesus. His propositions fail each time the believer responds rightly. Our Lord is faithful to His word.

Jesus addresses Martha's anxieties by sharing one simple profound truth, "only one thing is necessary". Jesus indicates that the one thing necessary is spending time with Him.

Taking Captives

My to-do list develops its own personality and breathes down my back for attention to add one more check mark. And my to-do list comprises good work that promotes the wellbeing of others. If writing and speaking to others about Jesus is my priority, but I fail to spend time with Him, then I miss the one necessary thing in fulfilling my calling. My good works are exactly that—mine.

Jesus wants me before my works. He wants me to be with Him before doing for Him. He knows that I need to possess strength and wisdom before serving. Otherwise, my efforts will lead to frustrations and telling Him what He should do with my work.

Everything competes for Jesus' status as necessary. We shift Him around like an appointment in our daily planner while contemplating what fits best in the time slot. Truthfully, Jesus occupying every time slot is the only position appropriate for Him.

Since taking the time to sit down and read a few

pages of this book, what other thoughts are attempting to interfere and distract you? Usually everything else that needs to be completed starts to invade. Laundry? Errands? Dinner? Children? Work? How do we silence the thoughts to make room for Jesus?

Disciplining our minds is a daunting task. To discipline our minds, we must be attentive to capture an intruding thought and put it to rest by subjecting it to Christ. Spiritual discipline is taking deliberate steps to guard, protect and grow in our relationship with Christ. Our thoughts are taken captive in obedience to Christ. We are responsible to take charge and make our thoughts behave as we do with our outward actions and responses. This means any negative thought will be countered with truth. One effective tip in dismissing the to-do list that seems to nag at us during our sacred moments is to write down the thought, and address it later. Your mind will not continue to circle in replaying your list repeatedly.

The goal is to manage distractions and be always sensitive to the presence of Jesus Christ's indwelling presence.

> *But when He, the Spirit of truth, comes, He will guide you into all truth; for He will not speak on His own initiative, but whatever He hears, He will speak; and He will disclose to you what is to come. He will glorify Me, for He will take of Mine and will disclose it to you.*
>
> *John 16:13-14*

Before we can serve another, we first require clarity to our mission in that we are serving Jesus Christ to others. We serve in His Spirit as ambassadors. Omitting this vital piece leads to avoidable consequences.

If not exercising sensitivity, many will become servants to demanding moments and neglect spending a quiet devotional time with Jesus. Moments become days; days become weeks; weeks become months; and unfortunately months become years. We find excuses to justify our behavior with statements such as:

- I'm too tired
- Not enough hours in the day
- On my way to work in the car is sufficient
- I listen to Christian radio
- God loves me anyway

We treat our most important relationship as careless as the McDonald's drive-thru window. Without speaking the words, our actions indicate that our time with God is as common as obtaining an Egg McMuffin, take it or leave it.

Our prayer life sounds something like, "I'll take a new job, more money in the bank, a better spouse with a side of help-me-get-through-this-day. And oh by the way, thank you. And to ease my conscience, here's a tip."

Of course, these previous sentences contain a little bit of playfulness and whole lot of sadness because they represent volumes of truth.

We receive the gift of life and use the gift as a means of blaming God for not having enough time. The amount of time is not the issue. It is how we choose to utilize the time. The choices we make define our time and our calendars reveal our values. Most of us would not dream of attending a wedding with a gift, then, declare the gift as insufficient for the bride and groom to enjoy. Each time we choose not to spend time with God, we re-direct His gift of time toward something that we deem more worthy. There will never be anything more important on earth than our relationship with Jesus Christ.

Jesus Christ deserves more than our on-the-go, anxiety-ridden lifestyles.

Relationships require concentrated time, effort, and energy to develop. Jesus Christ deserves more than our on-the-go, anxiety-ridden lifestyles. What does Jesus Christ deserve from us? He deserves our first fruits, our very best time and intention, and our full attention. Remember, His mind never wandered away from us on the cross. He remained fully engaged and faithful to the very end evident by asking for forgiveness on behalf of the crowd who carried out the actions responsible for His sufferings.

Jesus does not want Martha or us to worry or be bothered to the point of distraction that pushes aside His presence into the background. So, He takes the time to address the matter at hand directly. Jesus' words are impactful in delivering peace to a chaotic situation. The position for a believer is to take comfort in the fact that Jesus has overcome the world and its distractions (John 16:33). Peace from Jesus will override and dismiss distractions that arise from kitchens, marriages, relationships, employers, and so on by allowing your mind to order priorities appropriately.

For the believer, Jesus is always the number one priority. There is no situation, place, or person powerful enough to circumvent the peace that Jesus promises to believers. This peace comes with believing that Jesus is the Master of all including my time management. He will orchestrate every detail in due time, but I must first make Him a priority.

An encounter with Jesus will calm your troubled soul and teach you to receive each challenge with peace, strength, and grace—all undeserved gifts—as a result of a personal relationship with Christ and the indwelling Holy Spirit.

Charles Swindoll offers, "regardless of our difficulties, sufferings, and disappointments, focusing our minds on things that build our character will quench the flames of anxiety that otherwise fuel stress and disunity."[1] Jesus Christ, our personal Intercessor, builds our character as we choose to emulate His life as followers.

Just like Mary knew to sit at Jesus feet, to choose rightly, the Spirit will sensitize us to be in the right place where we belong. The Holy Spirit will bring to our attention and direct us to Jesus Christ. As we spend time with Him, we become sensitive to His leading, prodding, and teaching. We begin to learn His voice and words, but it only comes with spending time. We can identify fellow ambassadors when they visit with a timely message specifically for our encouragement. We see God fully while He remains a mystery to others. Developing a sensitivity to the presence of God keeps Him before us as we make critical decisions and responses. God is always with us. Let us commit to be fully present with Him, sitting, listening, and loving.

> *For the Lord will be your confidence and will keep your foot from being caught.*
>
> *Proverbs 3:26*

---

1 https://voice.dts.edu/article/lets-crown-character-in-todays-culture/ Voice.dts.edu/magazine DTS, pg 7, spring 2019. (Philip Yancey book quote)

Contemplation Corner

1. How do you describe your relationship with Jesus?

2. To whom do you identify the most? Mary or Martha? Both? Provide supporting details for your answer.

3. What is robbing you of spending precious time with Jesus?

4. What are some measures you can implement to protect your time with Jesus?

5. Before reading this book, had you considered your time with Jesus as precious?

6. How do you think Jesus views His time with you?

7. What are the benefits of spending time with Jesus?

8. How do you plan to spend time with Jesus? Be specific. Create a plan.

Chapter 8
Be Persistent

Read Mark 5:25-34

> After hearing about Jesus, she came up in the crowd behind Him and touched His cloak. For she thought, "If I just touch His garments, I will get well." Immediately the flow of her blood was dried up; and she felt in her body that she was healed of her affliction.
>
> *Mark 5:27-29*

I got myself in another situation. I have this tendency to commit to what sounds like a good idea and work out the details later. My mind latched on, and I became almost obsessed with getting it done. That happened when my friend suggested I train and run a half-marathon. Without any deep thought, I said yes to months of training, pain, discomfort, and bragging rights. Finally, the day arrived for my big event. I equipped myself with running essentials which included my cheering squad.

My dear friend gave timely advice for the run. "When you near the end of the race and start to feel pain, ask yourself this question: 'What does this pain have to do with me finishing the race?' And keep going".

I made a mental note and rehearsed the question silently. Sure enough with the finish line within reach, I needed the imparted wisdom to endure to the end. The results? I crossed the finish line, placed a checkmark on my list, and vowed… never to do that again.

The motivation to push past the pain point and continue forward was fueled by accomplishing a goal. Knowing what the finished line represented surpassed my will to give up. I mustered a surge of energy as I approached the end. The last bit of momentum multiplied providing strength to press on.

My half-marathon days pale in comparison to the woman who bled for 12 years. Her story is a true testament in staying the course despite setbacks and lack of physical or mental strength. She offers timeless tips in persistence transferrable to a much broader audience. Her will and strength while literally depleting remain strong enough to teach lifelong lessons. Her story which does not include a name remains applicable to anyone who is searching for wisdom in overcoming challenges with faith. She is the role model who does not permit others to have the final say in her condition. She moves forward amid obstacles to a greater solution with a heart filled with hope for healing.

Uncontrollable Circumstances

Circumstances that surface at the most inopportune times are annoying and often disruptive. Additional thoughts and plans are necessary to accommodate these unforeseen moments. Circumstances are not all negative. Some circumstances bring joy and laughter. We welcome these moments and the goodness that flows. When a negative circumstance approaches, we ready and prepare for the opposition. Rightfully so, we devise ways to remove ourselves or loosen the suffocating grip. We seek relief from the intensity that oftentimes leads to shallow breathing. We just do not wish to be bothered or entangled with such affairs. Sometimes we are responsible for the onset of the circumstances. Other times, the circumstances find their way to us on their own. Either way, we are susceptible to host unwanted and unplanned circumstances at any given time.

The bleeding woman experiences a circumstance which initially begins as a progression in natural female development. She reaches a celebratory point in maturation marking a defining moment in her life, a transitional moment. She will participate in the esteemed role of carrying and birthing life. She receives the circumstance, as most, with mixed feelings knowing that this change requires adaptation on her part to a new norm. She goes along with this natural progression and embraces her new status. In this instance, she encounters a positive circumstance that evolves into an unforeseen nightmare.

This specific circumstance which presents as a positive development that goes awry is not so uncommon. We experience these let down moments the day after childbirth (crying baby), the day after the wedding (bickering), the day after the job promotion (workload), the day after planting seeds in the garden (weeds). All these moments are glorious in a frozen frame, but what happens when the celebration ends, and an untamable reality begins. Persistence in thoughts and efforts become necessary to remain buoyant during the challenging times.

The bleeding began as a normal occurrence. However, there was nothing typical with this cycle. It did not end as anticipated. The bleeding lasted day after day for twelve long years. For what was created to be 5-7 days persisted for over 4,000 days.

At which point, did the situation become intolerable? Was it day 2,350? Humanly speaking, this experience had to be exasperating. No matter what task or appointment she accepted, in the back of her mind was a looming issue competing for attention. She was always thinking about how to accommodate this nuisance that was draining life from her body literally. This predicament consumed the woman physically, mentally, personally, financially, and spiritually. It overwhelmed her thoughts and attention with ideas that supported ridding her body of this nuisance. The honor was not worth the hassle.

As if her sufferings were not humiliating enough, she was stripped of the honor of sharing her personal name. Leaving the readers to identify her on the basis of her consuming ailment. The condition reshaped her identity and formed her reputation. Word spread within the community resulting in abandoning her name in exchange for the woman with a long-term bleeding issue. However, maybe the name was omitted intentionally so that one person's trauma can resonate with many others on a broader spectrum. Maybe the writer wants her name to be our names and her sufferings to serve as a guide to healing.

For others, the long-term circumstances may not be a bleeding issue. Many endure-long lasting situations which require an indescribable amount of effort with very little relief in sight. Hopeless marriages, rebellious children, illnesses, injuries, wrongful termination, childhood traumas, and so on. The pleading, begging, and questioning persist even to the point of blaming God who is the only hope. Life can be ruthless in derailing us, impeding progress with challenges you wished would just simply go away. The bleeding woman knew that her severe situation required more than wishing.

She carried the weighty burden of constantly reconciling whether to keep trying or simply give up. Habakkuk expressed similar frustrations when he cried out, "How long, O Lord, will I call for help, and You will not hear? I cry out to You, 'Violence!' Yet You do not save"(1:2). Deeply embedded in the suffering and witnessing no change, crying out appeared pointless. Yes, Habakkuk continued to seek God for an answer. Similarly, the bleeding woman maintained sufficient strength to question and continue trying one more time.

One More Attempt

Pain and suffering will drive you to seek relief from anyone who hints at relief. The bleeding woman does not sit idly by and accept her circumstances. She subjects her body to examinations and procedures that add to the discomfort. The discomfort is worth the potential healing. She visits many physicians allowing her body to become a case study, as her situation is not at all common amongst women. She appeals to their intellect and curiosity to solve this bodily mystery which has an independent stubborn will.

The physicians welcome an opportunity to observe this medical mystery at a price. The ignorance and unsuccessful treatments do not equate to free services. As the physicians participate in trial and error, the bleeding woman pays for their learning curve with hard earned resources. She relinquishes her last coins for potential relief from the burdensome pressure. The bleeding represents life draining from her body literally. She counters this imposition by seeking solutions that promise to restore life to her frail body. Physician after physician offer hope but fall short with making good on it. The emotional toll of ups and downs, month after month wears on her mental state. And yet, she finds the strength to seek out the next source.

> Outsider voices do not overpower the inner quiet whispers that echo, "Keep trying."

The drive to move forward meets complication at the hands of the ones who offer hope. The physicians think they can help her. She chooses to seek help from those who are more knowledgeable. What appears to be the good and right thing to do adds afflictions. She does not improve at all. In fact, her condition worsens. She becomes an experiment in the medical community. She endures the treatment while seeking deliverance. Maybe what the physicians learn will help another, but she is not there for that purpose. She is there to help herself first. This is the moment to give up on the dream for a fulfilled life.

To give up means to accept and learn to live with the physical and social limitations. The community views her as unclean and an outcast due to her illness. Those around her prefer her to live in the shadows, out of sight, and not participate in daily activities. Obstacles parade around her, offering reasons to fade in the background and resist pursuing a full, complete life. The community suggests that she accept a quiet death, allowing the grave to slowly take hold. The wishes of the community are formulated by a desire to ease their consciences of not helping someone in need.

Power is the ability to discover wisdom within and the courage to act on what it has to say.

Applying the adage, out of sight, out of mind to this situation means avoiding a commitment to suffer alongside another, shoulder the burdens of the weak, offer ways that will improve her life. The ease of looking the other way outweighs a humane response to another's suffering.

However, the outsider voices do not overpower the inner quiet whispers that echo, "Keep trying."

And she does. She keeps going, to the amazement of

all those watching. She proves that internal power does not exist by listening to outside noisemakers. Power is the ability to discover wisdom within and the courage to act on what it has to say. The outsiders surely ponder how does she find the strength to continue.

Hearing About Jesus

Years passed. The bleeding woman tried year after year to solve her problem. She subjected herself to experiments, examinations, and judgments. The will to continue dwindled slowly. Her drive and stamina were decelerating from the lack of progress. Fortunately, her crumbling remaining strength was adequate to pay attention to the community. The people were murmuring about a stranger who had the most intriguing reputation.

There was a mystery man named Jesus. He was no ordinary man. His works were unexplainable from a human reasoning standpoint. He fed 5,000 or more people with two fish and five loaves of bread. He was resurrecting the dead. The rumors said He must be from God because no other man healed a man born blind from birth. His healings were permanent and complete. No one recanted after encountering Jesus.

The only appropriate word to describe Jesus was extraordinary. His success rates surpassed the local physicians completely. In her mind she toyed with the idea of trying one more time. If the rumors were true, maybe Jesus possessed the remedy for her healing. He was answering prayers, restoring hope, and showing compassion for the afflicted. She thought maybe Jesus had enough compassion to address her situation. In all her trying, she never came close to this kind of power. It was treading upon unfamiliar territory.

> *The only appropriate word to describe Jesus was extraordinary.*

If the bleeding woman decided to move forward and take a chance, it would be no easy feat. Everyone wanted an audience with Jesus. She was just one surrounded by many. There was nothing unique about her amongst others with physical and spiritual needs. She was one tiny minnow in the vast sea of neediness. Jesus fascinated the hearts of numerous men and women who wanted an opportunity to just be near Him. The desire to be in the presence of remarkable power that cared about personal needs swept through the communities.

The woman had to find the courage to trust her mindset which had not failed her in the past with ideas. She needed a strategy to get close to Jesus in the company of others who had the same mission. The odds stacked solidly against her of reaching Him, but she had to try it. Jesus with an ironclad proven performance record was worth the risk.

Time to Act

The day arrived for the bleeding woman to act. Jesus was on the move performing miracles and delivering hope along the way. He was responding to a request from a synagogue official. Jairus begged Jesus to come and show mercy to his dying child. Jesus moved by the heartfelt sincere request and filled with mercy headed to Jairus' home. Others wanted to witness what mercy looked like in real life having not seen it in so long. Someone who cared about daily sufferings was making an impact. And a large crowd gathered and followed Jesus just to see with their very own eyes. They were persistent to satisfy their curious natures realizing their individual need for mercy as well.

The bleeding woman kept her mind focused on the fact that Jesus was in the vicinity, helping other poor desperate souls. The opportunity to seek Jesus for her need was now. She did not know His schedule or how long He planned to be in the area. All these factors prompted her to act on a belief that maybe Jesus had enough mercy for her too. She was drawn to seek help from a man who appeared greater than any man in her prior interactions. She could not permit her mind to wander off with the temptation to procrastinate. It was not the time to talk herself out of an idea. This was the time to grab hold of determination and run with it.

The large crowd presented a problem. But she had set aside a clean over garment for such purposes. As long as she kept her scarf near her face and with her sash hanging low in front, no one would notice her. And nobody would see her problem. At least not right away. It would give her the time she needed. Her mission was to get close to Jesus. If she was not able to secure a one-on-one meeting maybe the power extending from Him would be enough to cover her needs. She didn't have much time to overthink. She had to act. She fell in line with the crowd. They pushed. She moved forward. Having experiences with feeling uncomfortable were paying dividends at this moment. All the past trials and troubles strengthened her will as if serving as preparation for this precise instant. Caught up in the masses, feeling elbows in her sides, hands shoving her along were not a deterrent. She used these hurdles to propel her closer to her goal. She did not have time to give up. If ever she needed to rely on persistence, this was the time. Her eyes remained fixed toward her target and she inched forward.

Nontraditional Healing

She clung to the recurring purpose which kept her from walking away from the crowd. If anyone recognized her or sensed her bleeding trouble, they would certainly cry out. It was law, exactly like the one that said she had to remain a hermit until her bleeding ended. She set aside the fear and the past negative treatments and pursued the possibility that lay ahead.

Focus kept her from becoming annoyed with those in the crowd lingering without a sense of purpose, hanging around seeking entertainment. The number of people became irrelevant in her grand scheme. She maneuvered her way to blend in with the large crowd holding dearly to the pursuit of her purpose.

She thought, "If I just touch His garment, I will get well" (Mark 5:28). She knew in her depths that Jesus possessed the answer that eluded her grasp for so long. She was so sure of it. He was worth giving it a try one more time and seeking help for her problem that refused to nudge from previous interventions. Making her need known personally to Jesus seemed unlikely. She dismissed the idea of a private conversation settling for just a touch of the garment. Any touch point on the garment sufficed. With a simple touch, the bleeding woman expected to transfer her burdens to Jesus who appeared willing to lift the troubles and sufferings from the people.

She had learned about Jesus and contemplated His actions. She understood that this sort of power was not contained within a bodily form. She presumed that the body was incapable of housing such incredible power. Her conclusion led to a belief that the power extended past bones, skin, and tissue or clothing. She had nothing tangible on which to base her conclusion. No one was ever around her to confirm this thought and she certainly couldn't go to the temple. She relied on her faith to lead and guide her. She knew that faith helped her not to give up over the past twelve years. So, she trusted her faith again. She chose to lean not on her own understanding, but trust in God (Proverbs 3:5).

She envisioned the days filled with wellness once again. Uttering the words, "I will get well" bubbled joy. Believing the thoughts formulating in her mind energized her to take the next step toward her healing. She was so close, but so were others. Almost within reach, but not yet there. Reaching out but finding her arm pushed aside by others vying for position. Finally, the time arrived. This was as close as she was going to get. Stumbling forward and grasping for any parts of clothing that Jesus wore landed her fingers to scrape the bottom of His garment. She remembered her words, just touch His garment. The reaction time was immediate, instantaneous. She felt different. A feeling that evaded her for twelve years. The sense of wholeness swept through. Suddenly with the flow stopped, she sensed her perfect healing. She had waited for this event to occur day after day, year after year. And in one instance, she experienced an unexplainable power that caused healing just by getting close enough and reaching out to touch His cloak.

Jesus did not require undergoing a physical examination or consultation to understand her need. His power was like a blazing arrow which landed at its target with precision. The miracle left no room for second guessing or doubting what transpired. Jesus' healing power transferred in a manner that left no room for question. The transaction delivered an overwhelming deliberate statement of His willingness and ability to heal the hurting. This incomparable power overshadowed men and revealed limitations.

After exhausting the resources readily available to her, she sought God for an answer. God delivered her answer through His Son. God made it abundantly clear that man will always provide inadequate and imperfect solutions. Jesus can be trusted for timely and everlasting results accessible through faith.

Healing through Faith

Jesus, in complete awareness, sensed His power transferring to another. Surrounded by a large crowd, His attention began to search for the one. Many brushed up against Jesus on several occasions during this time. But someone touched Him that meant more than a mere brushing. Someone wanted something from Him that only He could provide. He sensed that someone was in the crowd who was willing to sacrifice personal interaction and settle for a touch instead. This person knew that a touch was all she needed. And Jesus wanted to know the person who had these thoughts about His great power.

Her touch caused Jesus to stop. He asked the question, "Who touched My garments?".

The disciples were puzzled by this question with so many people nearby. Their response was that many people had touched Him. It was impossible to single out one person in a crowd pressing in.

Jesus, unphased by the disciples' answer, looked around for the woman who touched Him. He refused to let her become swallowed by the crowd and fade into the background. He was not interested in treating her as the common society outcast. Jesus intended to bring that someone to the forefront and highlight the special trait that set her apart.

> *Jesus looked around to see the woman who had done this.*
>
> *Mark 5:32*

He gazed upon her inquisitively. The woman, perceiving that she was unable to escape His stare, stepped forward. Instinctively, she knew that Jesus was looking for her. She had no place to hide, no shadows to step into. She trembled with fear of the unknown but discovered the strength to approach Jesus. She fell down before Him and confessed the truth. Her posture indicated submissiveness, humility, and a sincere heart.

Jesus responded to her compassionately, "Daughter, your faith has made you well; go in peace and be healed of your affliction" (Mark 5:34).

Faith in Persistence

Jesus spoke directly to confirm the bleeding woman. His first word was to refer to her affectionately as daughter. Hearing this word, put her mind at ease and settled her trembling. Jesus wanted the bleeding woman to know that she chose rightly. And it was faith that led her to Him. Jesus also proved to be a rewarder of great faith. Her persistence got her close enough to touch

Jesus' garment. Her faith provided the fuel needed to move forward while encountering obstacles along the way. All the sufferings and disappointments were worth it in this moment. As she kneeled before her Lord, she received the words that she had longed to hear for over 12 years. Jesus' words instructed the bleeding woman to go and live in peace with her healing.

Interestingly, peace and healing accompanied one another. This healing returned her to an active role within society, silenced the ostracizers, and restored strength to her body. Jesus answered her prayers perfectly. She left home fractured from her long-term condition and returned whole, in peace. The search ended for another physician. The worries over resources in order to find a cure ceased. In one touch, she realized the life that was possible with Jesus.

God sent His Son with a potent message. "I came that they may have life, and have it abundantly" (John 10:10b). Jesus extended abundant life to a person who was losing life daily from blood loss. Stopping the blood was symbolic and confirmed in John 14:6, "I am the way, and the truth, and the life; no one comes to the Father but through Me." Jesus, true to His Words, provided life to a woman and conquered a condition that threatened to strip away life.

Throughout the bleeding woman's pursuit, one word

was missing from her actions—doubt. Not for one second did she doubt her healing would come from Jesus. There was no second guessing or feeling ridiculous for choosing to join the crowd. She exhibited confidence in the person she had heard about. The bleeding woman understood that doubting was self-defeating. Armed with the fact that doubting undermined her mission, she avoided the temptation. James wrote that anyone with doubts should not expect anything from God (James 1:6-7). With a made-up mind, she shut the door to doubting. Jesus was her only hope.

Healing and Peace

Jesus offered healing and peace to the bleeding woman.

His love and compassion are not just for the biblical pages but remain true for us today. As we search the world for many answers, Jesus wants us to understand that He is our only hope for restoration and peace. And the most exciting news is that He is willing to call us sons and daughters while performing miracles on our behalf.

The world is luring, attracting us to seek solutions within its borders. Empty promises parade around, drawing the eye in many directions. After following the world's lead and discovering a counterfeit deceitful plan to destroy us, we build our faith to follow Jesus. He prepares the way and walks alongside proving Himself to be trustworthy in every way.

The natural inclination is to spend time and resources figuring out life matters for ourselves. We are indwelt with self-centeredness which leads us to believe that we know what is best for us. The original sin wreaks havoc until we recognize its presence and destructive ways. At that point, we confront the truth. The truth is we are nothing without Christ. Our plans, marriages, children, careers are worthless without Christ. Self-centeredness will decrease over time as we mature in Christ but never dissipate in this lifetime. For this reason, Jesus even spoke about dying daily and crucifying self in order to truly follow.

> *And He was saying to them all, "If anyone wishes to come after Me, he must deny himself, and take up his cross daily and follow Me.*
>
> *Luke 9:23*

The bleeding woman walks away beaming in persistence and showcasing a new identity. Like Paul said in 2 Corinthians 5:17, "Therefore if anyone is in Christ, he is a new creature; the old things passed away, behold, new things have come."

The woman's experiences from thousands of years ago continue to lead us through crowds of distractors. Our mission is the same as hers, seek Jesus without shadows of doubt. Jesus will see us and heal our brokenness. Persistence is key to our spiritual growth which translates to peace. Be persistent in your pursuit of Christ.

Contemplation Corner

1. Is there a long-term problem that you are encountering?

2. Do you want to give up?

3. What keeps you moving forward?

4. Where do you turn to seek comfort and healing?

5. List the ways that you are persistent in pursuing Christ.

6. What role does faith play in your decision-making?

7. Do you believe that Jesus performs miracles today?

8. What do you want from Jesus? Will you fall down and confess before Him? Will you wait on the answer?

Chapter 9
Be Abiding

Read John 15:4-11

> *Abide in Me, and I in you. As the branch cannot bear fruit of itself unless it abides in the vine, so neither can you unless it abides in the vine, so neither can you unless you abide in Me.*
>
> *John 15:4*

Jesus speaks to listeners who are quite familiar with vines and branches. This horticultural region overflows in expertise pertaining to cultivating extraordinary vineyards. The intricate care for the vines and branches rewards growers with bountiful wholesome fruit. This common practice for the growers and partakers offers invaluable lessons to nurturing an intimate relationship into which Jesus desires for His followers.

For those of us who did not grow up around vineyards, appreciating this natural process, we may not grasp this analogy fully. Jesus suggests that a fulfilling relationship with Him requires understanding a vital connection like the one found in the vineyard. The vine keeper, vine, and branch intermingle in key roles to produce fruit.

The fruit represents the blessings that flow from the behind-the-scenes cooperative meticulous work. The fruit delivers sheer joy to the consumer, the observer and the participants responsible for the growth. Jesus inspires His followers to pursue a relationship with promises of inwardly and outwardly radiating joy.

Personally, this concept, *abiding*, became relevant after studying and increasing in knowledge about Jesus. Abiding was once not a priority, and the disastrous outcomes supported my ignorance. I experienced the consequences of leaning on the world which has a mission to ensnare hostages with misleading fear-based tactics. Conversely, abiding in Jesus strengthened my desire for self-control, especially for the small body part that can be highly destructive—the tongue.

Recalling an instance in not abiding, I overhead a conversation that included gossip regarding a friend. Without any thought on how this information would be received, I delivered the harmful words verbatim to my friend. This tactless effort backfired and cost me a friendship, severed for over thirty years. Unbeknownst to me, my friend struggled with this disparaging information, and to discover that her friends knew and discussed openly was too much for her to bear. She walked away from us, an immature, irresponsible group who behaved recklessly towards her.

Nothing in this scenario represented abiding in Christ. The fruit from this entanglement was ruined, discolored, and rotten to the core. There was no honor or glory to mention. Brutally hurt feelings and severed friendships were the results of abiding in self-righteousness.

> Self-control taught me to think before I speak.

Self-righteousness prevailed the moment I became caught up in the hype surrounding gossip. Not giving a second thought to another person's feelings or the potential damage, I marched forward possessed by the thrill of a juicy tidbit to share. The missing consideration for another led to a disregard for feelings, and potential consequences. I felt good in the moment, delivering this titillating news. However, the momentary thrill was not a panacea to the hurt propagated by my action.

Self-control taught me to think before I speak. Words spoken auditorily are difficult to retrieve after launch. I learned to adapt a minimalist lifestyle when it came to words and to attach each word to purpose before accepting or repeating it.

And through this experience and others, I have learned how to abide in Christ and what that means. In fact, there are many aspects of abiding in Him.

Intimacy

One prominent theme within the Christian faith is salvation. We trust and rely on our faith to save us from impending final judgment and damnation which is a fiery hell with complete separation from God. Belief in Jesus Christ provides eternal security assurance. "and I give eternal life to them, and they will never perish; and no one will snatch them out of My hand" (John 10:28).

Jesus settles this frightening fear by extending an invitation to follow Him. Every believer in Jesus Christ rests in this privilege that does not require any additional work beyond simple belief in Him as Savior. Paul confirms with "that if you confess with your mouth Jesus as Lord, and believe in your heart that God raised Him from the dead, you will be saved" (Romans 10:9). The relief and comfort that this promise brings settle future anxieties regarding eternal destination.

Another leading theme that receives less attention is the period between today and the ultimate destination. Jesus desires an ongoing relationship and a heart that depends upon Him for everything while we are alive on earth. Jesus' willingness to lay down His life and serve as the bridge to reconnect us to the Father indicates a godly purpose in daily living. Throughout Jesus' public ministry, His Words express intimacy with the Father. Expressions are prevalent, such as, "For I did not speak on My own initiative, but the Father Himself who sent Me has given Me a commandment as to what to say and what to speak" (John 12:49). These words scream intimacy. What Jesus has with the Father, He invites His followers to join and become active participants in this divine communion.

Intimacy requires an intentional, sacrificial commitment. Unfortunately, many will choose not to value this invitation and define life purpose within a godly context. The result is flailing or creating purpose without any substantial basis for support. Life becomes comparable to an elevator shaft without the elevator itself. The opening is there, but there's no connection. To link godliness with life and create meaning which bears bountiful fruit, Jesus says we need Him to accomplish this great feat. ". . . for apart from Me you can do nothing" (John 15:5b).

Spiritual Awareness

Living in a culture which ascribes to catchy slogans—be the best, captain of your own ship, master of fate, etc.—sends conflicting messages. *You can do all.*

You can be all. Really?

The point is not to extinguish the burning flame to succeed, but success without Christ is self-serving at best. Jesus makes it clear, without room for misinterpretation, that He is necessary for victorious living. If Jesus connects victory and success to Himself, the opposite indicates loss, failure, disappointment. Jesus holds authority over the world and its inhabitants. If we take a moment to view ourselves from a spiritual perspective and not permit the physical to be more appealing, we will conclude wholeheartedly with Jesus that nothing can be done apart from Him. Jesus possesses the plan and accessibility comes through Him.

Jesus makes the point clearly that nothing can be done without Him because so much is at stake. In this life, successes equate to material gain. But from a spiritual perspective, successes impact generations beyond view. Material gains endure pressures to invest, squander, inherit, hoard, protect and other worldly applications. Spiritual gains are not subjected to the worldly system. Spiritual gains sustain or multiply, but never subtract. Having no assigned ending or expiration dates, a spiritual understanding always works on behalf of believers starting now and into eternity. The benefits from spiritual versus material gains far outweigh the momentary pleasures, but this realization is only for the spiritual seeker.

Sustainability

Paul warns to be on guard against the flesh whose mission is to distract away from spiritual awareness.

> *For the flesh sets its desire against the Spirit, and the Spirit against the flesh; for these are in opposition to one another, so that you may not do the things that you please.*
> *Galatians 5:17*

For the believer, pleasing God is the number one priority in life. The things that please God include continuing the name and character of Jesus Christ throughout daily interactions.

The flesh has a mission to thwart all progress in pleasing God. This quest gains success by elevating a preoccupation with self. If I am constantly thinking about my prosperity, little time or energy will remain to focus on God or others.

Jesus models a completely different example for us to follow. His ministry is active in touching, healing, teaching, and pointing to the Father. Lasting success is built into this lifestyle model. Success from selfish gains increases your rankings in man's eyes but does nothing to fulfill spiritual satisfaction.

If feelings of restlessness, inadequacy, insecurities,

or confusion exist, these are absolute signs that an unhealthy imbalance is in play between the flesh and the Spirit. The Spirit assures "love, joy, peace, patience, kindness, goodness, faithfulness, gentleness, self-control" (Gal 5:22-23). This fruit overflows in abundance to the one who abides by communing through the Word and prayer.

Paying attention to your thoughts, feelings, and outward actions is an indicator that you are seeking to satisfy the Spirit rather than choosing to satisfy the flesh.

> *Watch over your heart with all diligence, for from it flow the springs of life. Put away from you a deceitful mouth and put devious speech far from you. Let your eyes look directly ahead and let your gaze be fixed straight in front of you. Watch the path of your feet and all your ways will be established. Do not turn to the right nor to the left; turn your foot from evil.*
>
> *Proverbs 4:23-27*

These wise words offer guidance on how to sustain and cultivate a gratifying relationship living in the Spirit.

Fleshly activities thrive upon creating distractions that draw away from God. And all too often, we conduct our lives in a way that welcomes these activities. Conversations, relationships, thoughts, and decisions appear to be harmless until the fruit reveals otherwise. Bickering, tension, and unhealthy interactions are indications of fleshly involvement. According to the natural law of cause and effect, each effect initiates from a cause. A godly or ungodly outcome does not appear suddenly. The effect begins to form with action initiated by the first thought, and the rest is history unless a course correction occurs. Applying this natural law to our behaviors and words, we raise awareness on how the flesh operates to intercept influences from God. John 15 offers abiding as key to denying the flesh an opportunity to wreak havoc.

The answer to standing firm against the flesh lies in abiding and trusting in the vine and vinedresser.

The answer to standing firm against the flesh lies in abiding and trusting in the vine and vinedresser. The vinedresser and vine operate with maximum efficiency and power that guarantee the branches bear sustaining fruit. The branch benefits from the unseen supernatural work. The vinedresser invests time and energy in this relationship for the long-term. This hands-on approach allows the vinedresser to become intimate in knowing the sensitivities and idiosyncrasies pertaining to growth. A vinedresser who spends one season with the vegetation is ill-equipped to speak intelligibly or lend expert advice on quality. For this reason, a vinedresser is known to spend decades with the vineyard, observing, adjusting, and nurturing to produce abundant fruit.

Just as the vinedresser has an acute interest in the

vine, the Father's obsession with His creation extends further. The branch receives from the vine and vinedresser. Their efforts cause the branch to produce irresistible fruit. The branch waits patiently for the nutrients to flow. The believer waits for a Spiritual infusion that impacts the heart. Fruit in a believer's life emerges from belief in the work Christ performed on the cross. The branch produces fruit as the believer waits for the Spirit to initiate a transformative work on the heart to love God above all else.

The Father-vinedresser, who desires glory, commits to this relationship to train and teach us how to bear fruit that pleases Him. Fruit that draws others to taste and marvel over its beauty. Attractive and appealing fruit with a luring effect.

> *O taste and see that the Lord is good; how blessed is the man who takes refuge in Him!*
>
> *Psalm 34:8*

The undergirding message that believers want others to know is that God is always good. God extends an invitation for all to come, touch, taste and experience His goodness. One bite from the fruit delivers everlasting refreshment for the soul. One answer to prayer has the power to redirect affections. And the Father-vinedresser smiles, for His labor and work, all done in love, reaches the beloved recipients.

Purpose

The abiding relationship clarifies purpose for the willing, submissive individual who enters this divine arrangement. Those who seek meaning and purpose in life find it in abiding alone.

People search for purpose to experience wholeness and meaningfulness. *How do I fit within this vast world? Why? What should I do?* A disinterest in the abiding relationship leaves one questioning, wandering, and searching for different methods to heal their brokenness and fill the hollow void. The wanderer is like the missing child who will not feel complete or safe until wrapped in loving parental arms once again. Everyone wants the same safe, secure home that Jesus occupies.

Sources outside the abiding relationship promise to provide answers to life-purpose by pointing to imposters/distractions such as careers, status, or other external self-efforts. Purpose lies with the Creator who holds the entire unique plan for the individual and universe. The divine plan covers from the beginning into infinity.

> *Great is the Lord, and highly to be praised, and His greatness is unsearchable.*
>
> *Psalm 145:3*

The most amazing aspect of the divine plan is man's incapability to duplicate or access it outside the realm of an abiding relationship. Embedded within the masterful plan is your name and your specific plan with excruciating details covering moment by moment of your earthly life span. Since no other source can compete at this magnitude, seeking sources outside the abiding relationship to gain insight into purpose is a meaningless and futile exercise.

The creative order specializes in purpose. Each aspect of creation plays a unique role in glorifying God. The stars, moon, vegetation, land, water, man, etc. glorify God and function within divine purpose in a unique way.

> *For since the creation of the world His invisible attributes, His eternal power and divine nature, have been clearly seen, being understood through what has been made, so that they are without excuse.*
>
> *Romans 1:20*

Passing by a tree swaying in a light breeze directs our thoughts higher than the gardener and ignites praise for such an astonishing thing. Regardless of how many times you pass the same tree, day after day, the glory of

God never reduces to a common occurrence. The role for all creation is to point to an almighty, all-wise God and celebrate His majesty.

> Personal purpose begins with understanding the Creator and seeking His will to experience success.

Once the pointing loses sight of a heavenly direction, perversion takes over by uplifting self. No other created thing deserves glorifying more than the Creator. In John 11, Jesus encourages Martha to believe so that she can see the glory of God, an appealing proposition (40). Nourishing your beliefs by reading and studying maintains focus on a lofty, spiritual placement.

Personal purpose begins with understanding the Creator and seeking His will to experience success. Paul prays for the Colossians to "be filled with the knowledge of His will in all spiritual wisdom and understanding" (1:9). Paul knows that this knowledge is necessary to strengthen godly purpose which travels through a direct conduit from Jesus Christ.

Dependence

An abiding relationship establishes a trustworthy context for how to maneuver life. One emphasis is not to try and do it alone. Man, as a created being, is not equipped to live independently in isolation. The need for social interaction and connectivity defines livelihood. There is a major difference between existing and living. Social isolation leads to depression, poor immune systems, and other mental health challenges. The reason for this reaction is due to humanity's intrinsic design to be active in relationships. And the first relationship that demands attention and takes precedence is with God. Sadly, God often becomes the last resort as if an afterthought. When in fact, as part of our creative design, we are to be in a dependent, loving relationship with God.

> *And my God will supply all your needs according to His riches in glory in Christ Jesus.*
>
> *Philippians 4:19*

Needs include oxygen, food, shelter, water, and all the life-sustaining elements. We need God for the very air we breathe. We are created fearfully and wonderfully to depend on Him for our every need. We grow to know Him as a loving Father who cares about every single detail, no matter how small or large. This dependency leads to confidence which strengthens faith.

An honest contemplation over your life, past and present, should yield overwhelming evidence of God's activity in moving on your behalf. Pertinent moments that are humanly unexplainable will show up in the recollections—a sudden shift, an answer to prayer, the heavens open after periods of waiting. We experience His provisions and protection promises while overlooking the love behind each occurrence. God remains true to His commitment even as His creation rejects Him for a lesser god. Thankfully, His love for us is not dependent upon our actions. Inherent in His nature is this unfathomable love and desire to be in a relationship with us even as we behave as wayward teenagers. His abiding love stands the test of time and never fails to be ever present working on our behalf.

Fruitfulness

The proof or evidence of a life that abides in Christ is what John refers to as fruit. As the vinedresser and vine work in sync with the branch to produce delectable fruit, so does God the Father and His Son Jesus interacts with the believer. The delight is to overwhelm the branch with ripe nutritious fruit that appeals to others to admire and partake. Upon notice of such bountifulness, seekers marvel in amazement at a phenomenal sight. Such is the description for believers as well. Our inextinguishable light shines brightly, warming the most stubborn-hearted to inquire. Ripe tender fruit occurs from surrendering and becoming a willing participant with the Father and Son. This relationship restores believers' hope in the original intent for creation. As this interaction occurs, a desire to be holy, pure, righteous, and loving are supernatural outputs. The overflow from this relationship draws others to examine the traits that set apart the believer. Christlike traits that are bewildering to the unbeliever. The believer simply knows and accepts the life results as bountiful fruit that grow out of this precious spiritual relationship.

Subscribing to a lifestyle that welcomes godly instructions and direction experiences smoother sailing during the rough patches. Knowing that you are not alone and that God promises to work all situations out for your own good ushers in an indescribable peace during challenging times. The unwanted life pressures are not as intimidating and fearful because your help never leaves. He carries you through while continuing to implement the plan that He has for you.

Jesus confirms His power to overcome any threat that targets a believer's path. The ultimate proof lies in Jesus demonstrating His authority over life. Resurrecting Lazarus from the tomb in which he resided for four days, sends a clear message that Jesus is the victor over death (John 11:43). By removing the fear of death (the worse threat the evil one can throw), we are free to live a fruitful life that bears witness to the kingdom of God.

Jesus extends an invitation to join perfection for immeasurable life results that bring honor to His name. An individual relying on his own cognition and ideas collides with self-limiting boundaries. Aligning and abiding with divinity means exponential growth, abundance, and assurance. Specifically, abiding takes an interest in the heart condition. Bitterness, resentment, and coveting are emotions that will impact the fruit. The vinedresser will not spare any attention to details to avoid results in poorer quality. An abiding relationship exercises laser focus into the heart to sweep away any negativity that impedes progress in mirroring Christ. A heart free of pesky internal distractions enjoys freedom in glorifying and worshiping as goodness and love flow to generously bless others.

Abiding is an all-consuming offer that warrants a complete commitment. Showing up half-heartedly produces fruit of smaller proportions, bruised markings, or no fruit at all. No one will be interested in inquiring about your fruit. They won't consider you a source of reliable produce. You will be passed up for a more appealing vineyard leaving the vinedresser with a marred reputation from your example. This life remains idle with a poor connection to purpose or fulfillment comparable to stagnant water. The evidence of this condition will be the lack of curiosity or pursuit by others. The mindset shows little to no interest in spiritual matters since thoughts are held captive by the physical. A half-hearted effort leans towards satisfying the flesh.

Examining Jesus' life and examples, His actions represent whole-heartedness towards His followers. A commitment to this abiding relationship requires your mind, heart, and body. Divine lessons will flow through the whole you to produce a marvelous fruit for others to taste and consume divine nutrients. And this truth leads to a life well lived with no regrets.

Fruit is the word or action that anchors in honoring or displaying God's attributes. The proof is in the pudding. Do you season your words with Christ? Can I hear Christ extending an invitation to the weary from listening to you? What is the answer or hope for your salvation or freedom?

Serving others with a heart disinterested in selfish recognition or gain, but with intentions to point to the Source of your strength dribbles pebbles for others to follow along. The Father loves Jesus. Jesus loves his disciples. Jesus simply invites His disciples to abide in His love (John 15:9). Love becomes the predominant characteristic for an abiding life. Love for the Father, love for the Son, love for the believer to experience a life worthy of the call.

Three prominent themes permeate through this

passage: abiding, bearing fruit, and glorifying God. These themes highlight a pattern for us to trace.

In cutting fabric, we lay the pattern on top of the fabric and trace. The result is a duplicate of the pattern. If we lay on top of this divine pattern, the result for our lives will be an image of God's Son confirming Romans 8:29, ". . . predestined to become conformed to the image of His Son."

The fruit from this decision will be an extension of Christ and His character—a life that continues to move in compassion, love, joy, peace, and desiring the very best for others. This life lays down fear by realizing the true satisfying power that is available in an abiding relationship. The person who chooses the superior abiding lifestyle knows this divine connection offers godly simplicity, sincerity, and success.

In the abiding relationship, the vinedresser receives the accolades. The branch relies on the vine and the vinedresser to flourish. This is an interdependent relationship that rises to excellence when all aspects align and work together with a common mission. Neither the vine, branch, nor the fruit objects to the vinedresser's treatment. This trusting relationship understands that wisdom belongs to the vinedresser and submits willingly. The branch accepts the lesson that Jesus teaches Martha as she mourned the death of her brother.

Jesus said to her, "Did I not say to you that if you believe, you will see the glory of God?"

John 11:40

God's glory is a marvelous wonder to witness.

Contemplation Corner:

1. What appeals to you most about an abiding relationship?

2. What are the results of living outside an abiding relationship?

3. What does it mean to you that apart from Jesus you can do nothing?

4. How often do you attempt to start without Jesus?

5. Why was it necessary for Jesus to teach the concept of abiding to His disciples?

6. Why is it necessary for you to learn as much as possible about abiding?

Chapter 10
Be About Your Father's Business

Read Luke 2:40-49

> *His mother said to Him, "Son, why have You treated us this way? Behold, Your father and I have been anxiously looking for You."*
>
> *And He said to them, "Why is it that you were looking for Me? Did you not know that I had to be in My Father's house?*
>
> *Luke 2:48-49*

Showing up to write the final chapter, everything is in order to welcome productivity. Careful attention to the lighting, temperature, external noises, and a stern warning to others not to disturb me unless the house is on fire creates my ideal environment. However, other visitors are present, lurking around to extract the pleasure from productivity. Facebook, text notifications, phone calls, and e-mails are unwanted intruders. I have the power to shut them out as well, but do I? These time busters arrive to tease and test my discipline. I imagine these thieves celebrating and rejoicing over their win at my expense. Their success in impeding my progress is a deadline extension on my part. If they win, that means I admit defeat. Again.

In an age complete with busyness and distractions, we tend to struggle with focus and intentionality. Our calendars and daily schedules shuffle priorities to the end of the day or not at all. Jesus, at a young age, seems to display a firm grip on the things that matter. Something or Someone captures his attention to the exclusion of everything, including parents, for three whole days. Fascinating to this passage is Jesus being away from home during this time without concern for comforts or familiarity. To Jesus, creating the perfect setting such as lighting and temperature is as unnecessary as a fan on a blistery winter's day. From an early age, commitment to His life mission continues to instruct others on how to love and serve God well.

Duty Calls

Joseph and Mary were dutiful parents careful to observe and live according to Jewish traditions. Attending the Feast of the Passover was a protected event in their schedules that occurred annually. Timely preparations for the anticipated journey progressed as a testament to commitment. Certainly, obstacles appeared before or during the trip. Nevertheless, Joseph and Mary joined in commemorating Passover and celebrating a major deliverance feat by God. Like most committed Jews of the day, raising Jesus in the faith was a priority for their home. Surely his divine nature showed, and they had clearly been told who He was, yet they waited for the proper age to share the Feast and its meaning with Him.

Jesus was growing in wisdom shepherded by the grace of God. In these few verses, the Scriptures painted a picture for us to understand the vital importance of creating structure and setting godly priorities within the home. Learning and growing in faith appeared to be part of natural life developments such as crawling, walking, eating, and reading. Knowing and loving God were a natural progressive development trend as if it belonged on the pediatrician checklist which measured growth at each visit. Joseph and Mary provided invaluable insight on establishing a home built on focus and intentionality.

Jesus, the Exception

Jesus demonstrates an uncanny ability to shut out the surrounding world completely. Many will argue that Jesus has a divine advantage to focus, commit, and love without hesitation. Jesus is the exception with His holy nature and ability to communicate with the Father so freely. This belief has truth in it but not to the point of us giving up on desiring to be more like Christ. The thoughts that encourage us to settle for personal weaknesses give an excuse not to yearn for holiness. These thoughts originate from within the enemy's influence. A temptation to use Jesus' divine nature as an excuse not to model His example signifies a lack of understanding of the power available to believers through faith.

True, Mary gives birth to a child who is like none other, God-Man in the flesh. God-Man means Jesus is fully God and fully Man. He is 100% God and 100% man, an unsolvable math equation but perfect theology! Jesus is a Savior who identifies with mankind in every way except sin.

> *For we do not have a high priest who cannot sympathize with our weaknesses, but One who has been tempted in all things as we are, yet without sin.*
>
> *Hebrews 4:15*

Our weaknesses are Jesus' strengths in which He completes and prepares us to commune with our holy God. Before Jesus undertakes His mission to mankind, one prominent quality exists that fosters His commitment. Jesus unequivocally loves the Father, and His mission is for us to love God too. Jesus is the exception. And this fact alone qualifies Him as God.

After spending quality time fulfilling obligations at the Passover, Joseph, Mary and the caravan began traveling home. Certain that everyone understood the departure schedule, the need for a role count seemed unnecessary. After journeying for a day, Jesus' missing presence became evident. The searches began to no avail. The return to Nazareth was not a pressing need for Jesus. He remained behind in Jerusalem attending to more important matters.

As Jesus matured, His participation in Feasts was expected. What was unexpected was His divine insight which caused those with knowledge to marvel and ponder. Jesus amazed teachers and others listening with wisdom beyond his years. Jesus fully engaged this group for three days to the disregard of any other person or commitments on His part. The interaction was so enthralling to the participants that no one asked, "to whom does this child belong?" Their minds and hearts were so enraptured with the subject matter and in-depth expressions until nothing was worthy of disruption.

As with any parent desperately trying to locate a missing child, panic set in during the search. Upon returning to Jerusalem with considerable time passing, finding Jesus was a relief. But soon relief gave way to puzzling thoughts. Of all places, Jesus was discovered at the temple. Finding Him interacting with much older, seemingly wiser adults with a keen concentration on His words mystified his parents. A young lad, who just earned the privilege to attend religious feasts, commanded the attention of adults well versed in the Scriptures. What has taken them years to understand, Jesus expounded with ease and divine mastery. And in the discussion, Jesus imparted wisdom and additional insights that stunned the listeners. Their engagement which began as a brief encounter lasted for days without any weariness or complaints expressed. Each person regarded Jesus' presence as an inexplainable heart- and mind-captivating experience.

Immediately disregarding the gathering, Mary approached Jesus for an explanation. After days of searching for a missing child, comfort existed only in laying eyes and hands on her boy. Such an unthinkable act demanded an explanation. "Son, why have You treated us this way?" (Luke 2:48) were the first words that expelled from Mary.

These were reasonable words from any parent expressing disappointment in a child's decision. Jesus, true to His mission and utmost dedication responded inquisitively to His mom, "Did you not know that I had to be in My Father's house?" (Luke 2:49).

Did you not know? No. Joseph and Mary did not

know. The far-reaching magnitude of the words delivered by an angel who declared that Mary was with child escaped their humanly comprehensive grasp. Unbeknownst to His parents, one day Jesus would seize the opportunity to further expound upon the angel's intent. Jesus clarified that His devotions and passions stretched beyond earthly parents to a heavenly realm. And this divine relational position could never be reversed, transformed, or challenged. Mary and Joseph's parental power fell in subjection to an active holy alliance in place before Jesus' earthly entrance. The parents were blessed to be reunited with Jesus, and yet bewildered by his response. Joseph, Mary, and Jesus returned home to continue nurturing this exceptional Child fathered by the Holy Spirit.

Exceptional Way

At any given instance of engaging Jesus in the Bible, you will find Him being about His Father's business. From an early age, the allegiance is clear, and the focus never changes from pre-birth to post-Cross. All words, mannerisms, and motivations lead to the Father. Accepting this truth underscores a greater meaning to Jesus's own words.

"I am the way, and the truth, and the life; no one comes to the Father but through Me."

John 14:6

The bottom line is we need Jesus. We need His words, teachings, examples, life, and death because through it all, He reveals the Father to a hungry and thirsty world that implodes and exasperates without Him. And apparently, this knowledge is far superior to anything the world promotes. If we accept the cruciality of knowing the Father, our minds, actions, and entire approach alter in order to be about the Father's business just like Jesus.

Choosing alignment with the world leads to mediocrity and giving up on the hidden undeveloped potential within God-given talents.

An exceptional life is available to all. However, exceptionality does not dwell amongst worldly influences. The enemy actively seeks to discourage the pursuit of an exceptional way and promotes ignorance over awareness. Completely unaware of the consequences of this mindset, we end up abiding in poverty accepting a below-average threshold for living. Choosing alignment with the world leads to mediocrity and giving up on the hidden undeveloped potential within God-given talents. The Father becomes irrelevant and outdated. This thinking accepts wisdom as archaic, offering no trustworthy applications to the current lifestyle, even though Ecclesiastes 1:9 reminds us that there is nothing new under the sun.

This reckless thinking fails to realize that the God of Adam is our faithful God too, unchanging and lavishing us with His love even while undeservingly.

The enemy's method involves enticing us to specialize in creating our own form of human wisdom. Next, he emboldens us to spread these false ideals and half-truths amongst friends or anyone else who lacks discernment. The intoxicating words are as effective as overripe peaches to fruit flies.

Human wisdom derives from a reservoir which contains lessons from personal experiences and knowledge. The problem resides in imperfect perceptions and interpretations from a singular lens through which to draw conclusions.

Trusting in God provides access to a full spectrum that applies to our circumstances and perfectly reflects on His goodness and mercy. An option is always available to choose divinely-inspired, proven principles that deliver guidance for rightful living every single time. Following Jesus protects us from the enemy as he seeks to alienate us from the Father and upholds a false shield that obstructs our clear heavenly vision. Believers enjoy protection from the enemy's plots by employing God's power as protection by utilizing faith (1 Peter 1:5).

Being before Doing

The mistake many make is to begin doing before being. We find Jesus and the thrill of this discovery propels us to serve Him with actions. As much as hands and feet are needed to serve and proclaim the gospel, it tarnishes the mission without adequate preparation.

Preparations begin with being. Doing provides an opportunity for the evil one to run interference with our calling. The first calling for every believer is an invitation to first come, be and rest in a divine Presence who has been waiting patiently. Satan does not want this interaction or relationship to occur, let alone progress. The spiritual riches and power available are sufficient to overcome the devil and his influences. Unleashing these riches and power depends on *being* with God to gain assurance and confidence in His love for us. Otherwise, God's offerings remain unnoticed or unappropriated.

So, the enemy operates in demonic schemes to temporarily intercept God's plans for his own sake. The ultimate mission is to create various scenarios that draw us away from this ideal place to be, with God.

Being with God means stilling ourselves before holiness and perfection while submitting to Him as

Creator with complete authority. "Cease striving and know that I am God" (Psalm 46:10). Being is finally returning home after spending time away attempting to fill the void with meaningless substitutes. It means expressing joy and relishing in the relationship and salvation that a loving Father provides. Being with God is a first-hand encounter with grace, mercy, and forgiveness along with many other divine attributes. This sacred place is where the foundation for the love of God is set, formed, and multiplied. The heart becomes softer and pliable allowing God to massage and shape it towards Himself.

> **Being is the place set aside designed especially for the weary to come, rejoice, and remain strengthened.**

Being with God is where we discover the shortcomings in our character. Here, we meet substance and develop a sour taste towards superficiality. In His presence, we wrestle with falling in love with Jesus until overcome by His unfailing devotion. We accept the realization that Jesus' love for us and the Father is simply matchless. And no other thing or person will ever reach the deep crevices in our souls and satisfy the longings to be loved in this manner. The psalmist describes this desperate feeling as, "As the deer pants for the water brooks, so my soul pants for You, O God. My soul thirsts for God, for the living God; when shall I come and appear before God?" (Psalm 42:1-2). And most importantly, we gain a vision for the one day when we live in a sinless perfect state permanently. Unburdened, unbothered, and unbroken by the enemy's pastime activities to harm, we find rest. Being is the place set aside designed especially for the weary to come, rejoice, and remain strengthened.

Foregoing this state of *being* in order to scurry onto *doing* results in cracks in the spiritual foundation. Mindlessly, our impulsivity creates opportunities for the enemy to slip in and deceive. We leave God behind and send messengers urging Him to hurry and catch up with our program. The divine order switches and somehow, we possess all the solutions for God's kingdom.

To be about God's business, we must first commit to being with Him. Jesus expresses this principle as He often pulls away from the crowds to pray and be alone with the Father.

Being about the Father's business requires intentional focus. I recall listening to a random Christian program and the speaker mentioned that one day Jesus will return. How did my daily activities sideline this basic tenet of the faith?

Christ's return gives hope and courage to those waiting. But with an over-packed schedule, powerful truths drift to a faraway place without immediate access.

Unfortunately, we permit what matters most to collect cobwebs and dust as we carry on with meaningless tasks.

The only feasible solution in overcoming spiritual misalignment is to choose God and make Him a priority each day. God belongs at the core.

The core in the body holds power, strength, and stability. An athlete pays careful attention to this area to combat fatigue and poor posture. Proper alignment positions the body to experience success in athletic endeavors. In the long run, a strengthened core is responsible for impacting endurance, efficiency, and protection from injuries.

The same reigns true for believers. With a strong spiritual core emphasis, God's influence extends to all aspects of life. The diagram below illustrates how spiritual strength is necessary in feeding and sustaining wholeness.

With God as the prominent core occupant, spiritual truths and wisdom flow freely and become easily accessible.

A weak core that relies on other unworthy sources is incapable of meeting untimely demands with confidence. Illnesses, disappointments, arguments, and unanticipated setbacks do not occur on a schedule.

Preparation to meet whatever life brings your way begins with strengthening and building upon the core. The core becomes stronger by engaging in activities that support knowing God and applying that knowledge daily. Just as building muscles require time, consistency and repetition so does spiritual endurance. Rushing through and skipping essential exercises yield predictable results, weaknesses and injuries. A daily dose of discipline trains the body and mind where to seek guidance, direction, knowledge and how to respond to trials successfully. This practice protects us from leaning on our own understanding.

Paul emphasizes discipline repeatedly in the Bible. "Do you not know that those who run in a race all run, but only one receives the prize? Run in such a way that you may win. Everyone who competes in the game exercises self-control in all things. They then do it to receive a perishable wreath, but we an imperishable" (1 Corinthians 9:24-25). Self-control, another word for discipline, equips one to receive Christ and appropriate Him throughout each moment of the day.

A primary benefit of strengthening the core is experiencing true freedom. Freedom and abundance are two of the many gifts that Jesus offers His followers.

> *The thief comes only to steal and kill and destroy; I came that they may have life, and have it abundantly.*
> *John 10:10*

A free believer moves in sync with Jesus while avoiding danger zones. Even with a miscalculation and finding yourself in the middle of danger, trusting in Jesus is the primary strategy for deliverance. "Yet those who wait for the Lord will gain new strength; they will mount up with wings like eagles, they will run and not get tired, they will walk and not become weary" (Isaiah 40:31). Freedom invades the whole being so that worship flows from mind, body, and soul freely.

The opposing alternative is bondage. ". . .for by what a man is overcome, by this he is enslaved" (2 Peter 2:19b). The enemy seeks to overcome and overwhelm by gripping with fear. Bondage reveals itself through anger, rage, despair, insecurities, and other draining emotions. Whereas God is the source for a strengthened core, self intervenes with a prominent role in knowing what is best. Since self is incapable of knowing what is best, the abundant life shrinks to unforgiveness, bitterness and a less than desirable life trapped by the enemy in a darkened stupor.

Be About the Father's Business – Falling in Love

Christ does not function in a legalistic role but one in which His Spirit is active in making His love known to us and through us. Peter writes to believers, "and though you have not seen Him, you love Him, and though you do not see Him now, but believe in Him, you greatly rejoice with joy inexpressible and full of glory" (1 Peter 1:8). The Bible reads as one long love letter containing a message from the Lover that He will never let go. His pleasure for creation is unending celebratory elation.

David says, "Surely goodness and lovingkindness will follow me all the days of my life, and I will dwell in the house of the Lord forever" (Psalm 23:6). Goodness and lovingkindness aka mercy are two faithful travel companions who accompany believers everywhere. Their presence is impossible to escape. Any attempts to run away result in a high-speed chase from these two companions who refuse to leave a believer alone.

The blood that Jesus offers comes with a simple condition, believe. No matter how grievous the sin or waywardness, God's love is more than enough to cover and restore. This love which knows no restraints draws believers closer. Getting to know God and understanding His love is essential to being about the Father's business. Accepting God's love for this world then taking the next step to personalize that love is humbling.

It is challenging for the selfish minds and hearts to comprehend an act that is the epitome of selflessness. The Father chooses to humiliate His Son on a vile cross to extend an offer to His enemies. And while Christ hangs on the cross, my name and your name appear for the future time that we will need this offer. The perfect plan moves in perfect love for an imperfect people.

Now, that is love.

Before you can be about the Father's business, experiencing His love as a sacred romance is a necessity.

The Father's Business

My role in the Father's business is spending quality time in getting to know Him. Knowing God is an intimate relational experience. As we grow in knowledge and understanding, our hearts reflect His divine nature. We transform into a living witness for His name. The opportunity to share God's goodness without reservations or doubts becomes the new normal for our lives. Coupling knowledge with belief is a godly transaction which ignites a fiery curiosity that extends into a lifetime of learning and sharing. The heart grows full and overflows to others in immeasurable volumes. However, the believer reflects only a fraction of the pure love that God possesses. Unable to wholly express all of God's love due to our fallen sin-tainted natures, we experience frustrations with our limitations. To overcome this tension, we strengthen our faith in what we know to be true and in whom we love.

The Father is highly relational. In Genesis 2, The Lord walks "in the garden in the cool of the day" (8) for an opportunity to spend time with Adam and Eve. Genesis 1:18 shows God declaring, "It is not good for man to be alone; I will make a helper suitable for him". God provides Eve to serve as a physical companion, helper for Adam. He avails Himself as the perfect spiritual companion, a helper for Adam and believers. God loves togetherness and expects fellowship with creation as a natural occurrence. He expresses one of His many love languages through quality time.

This pure love oftentimes meets our insatiable fleshly cravings that attempt to prosper through selfish gains. We rush in, drop our requests, and rush out leaving behind a hurting God who waits tolerantly to hear our impure motives. God who defines healthy relationships by quality time knows the individual's heart. He feels the ripple effect from affections that lean toward the world more so than Him. Partaking in the Father's business includes understanding how vital relationships are to Him. Spending time with the Father is non-negotiable. The time commitment is not only out of necessity but also to return love to the Father. Otherwise, there is no legitimate business dealings with Him.

> *See how great a love the Father has bestowed on us, that we would be called children of God; and such we are. For this reason the world does not know us, because it did not know Him.*
>
> *1 John 3:1*

Just as Adam and Eve encountered sweet fellowship in the Garden, our main priority is to show up with expectancy for the same. Trusting that God has the capacity to love all collectively and individually, He meets us personally and calls our name. His calling is a longing to spend time with us. A desire to be near God, whether meditating, praying, or studying His Word, delivers joy to our Creator.

> *Behold, I stand at the door and knock; if anyone hears My voice and opens the door, I will come in to him and will dine with him, and he with Me. He who overcomes, I will grant to him to sit down with Me on My throne, as I also overcame and sat down with My Father on His throne.*
>
> *Revelation 3:20-21*

Jesus' offer to dine means fellowship and vibrant conversations with a sense of heavenly belonging. Being in God's presence is the only place to find wholeness, stillness, and perfect peace.

The Father's business requires us to shut out the world and become enthralled with Him. Our conversations, lifestyle, relationships, and choices all reflect divine intimacy. We speak from a vantage point as ones who have inside knowledge. We know Him not only as Father, but 'our Father,' employing possessive pronouns. Frequent intentional private times with God shapes the heart to find purpose for life in Him. As believers, we realize that nothing that excludes God is worthy of our focus. Jesus' question becomes our question.

> *"Did you not know that I was about my Father's business?"*
>
> *Luke 2:49*

Contemplation Corner

1. Have you ever lost track of time while engaged in godly matters?

2. How do you protect yourself from worldly influences overshadowing a godly perspective?

3. Do you agree that a spiritual emphasis at the core feeds into other areas?

    a. If so, how successful are you in each area? Which area could use improving?

    b. If not, how are you choosing to nourish each area?

4. What does the Father's business mean to you?

Thank you so much for purchasing/reading my book. I would love to stay in touch and hear from you. There are several different ways for us to build upon this relationship:

#1 Visit my website, displaystrength.com, and sign up for the newsletter. You will receive a free pdf download as a gift.

#2 Send me an email. Share questions or progress concerning your spiritual growth.

#3 Follow me on Instagram, @gwen_burno.

#4 Reach out if you are interested in learning more about my coaching or speaking,
calendly.com/coachgwen/30min.

#5 Pray that God will continue to use my life as a light to help others see and love Him.

Until next time,
Gwen

Acknowledgments

A special thanks to Roaring Lamb Ministry for committing to a mission that encourages Christians to write. The workshops, conferences, newsletters, and personal support paved the way to completing this book. I am grateful to be a recipient of your many blessings.

My heart overflowed with gratitude from the moment I met Marji Laine, editor. I cried. God sent someone who understood and radiated patience and grace, a couple of her many virtues. Marji poured into me this entire project. Her edits, questions, and suggestions pushed me to be better. Your love for the Lord ensured that we represented Him well in our thoughts and written expressions. May God continue to overwhelm you with His blessings so that others may experience Him through you.

And most importantly, thank you to my Lord and Savior, Jesus Christ. Writing this book with You led us into some unexpected places. I loved the moments when the words were clearly Yours and not mine. I clung to You in the valley until I learned the lesson that this book is for Your namesake and not mine. You reiterated over and over the importance of following and not leading. You were my faithful good Shepherd in writing this book.

My prayer is for the love relationship between Jesus and myself stir many hearts to fall in love as well. “Greater love has no one than this, that one lay down his life for his friends” (Jn 15:13).

About the Author

Gwen Burno is the founder of Wisdom & Wellness LLC, an organization that provides sound principles and strategies which equip others to pursue a well-ordered life. In this capacity, she serves as a Certified Christian Life Coach, Certified Equipping Profile Coach, Ramsey Financial Coach, and Speaker who helps others to move forward in decision-making with boldness, confidence, and courage. She loves helping professional Christian women win mentally and financially through God-centered feedback and clinically-proven resources.

Gwen places a premium on higher education having spent a considerable amount of time pursuing academic interests. She holds a Bachelors of Business Administration degree from Georgia State University, Masters of Business Administration from Alaska Pacific University and a Masters of Arts in Biblical Studies from Dallas Theological Seminary. She teaches a weekly adult women Bible class in which the participants are challenged to think through biblical truths and commit to implementing these principles into practice. She is a contributing writer in Stories of Roaring Faith, Volume 3. Her passion is helping others reduce stress and anxiety by living intentionally according to biblical principles and a personal relationship with Jesus Christ.

She resides in Dallas with her husband (Rowland) and three adult children (Jeremy, Mikaela and Kiersten).

Gwen Burno

Certified Christian Life Coach | Ramsey Financial Coach | Speaker, Author

www.displaystrength.com gwen@displaystrength.com

972-886-8370

www.ingramcontent.com/pod-product-compliance
Lightning Source LLC
Chambersburg PA
CBHW071322090426
42738CB00012B/2764
* 9 7 9 8 9 8 7 2 7 7 9 0 4 *